THE UNANSWERED QUESTIONS OF SCIENCE

EXPLORING THE MYSTERIES OF OUR UNIVERSE

SHIVAM GOEL

Dedication:

To my parents, who always encouraged my curiosity and love for science. Your unwavering support and belief in me have been instrumental in my pursuit of understanding the mysteries of our universe. This book is dedicated to you both.

Contents

Foreword

Foreword:

Science has been instrumental in advancing our understanding of the universe we inhabit, from the smallest subatomic particles to the largest cosmic structures. Despite the remarkable progress we have made, there are still many unanswered questions that continue to elude our grasp. It is this thirst for knowledge and the pursuit of answers that drives us to explore the mysteries of our universe.

In "The Unanswered Questions of Science: Exploring the Mysteries of Our Universe," the author takes us on a captivating journey through the most intriguing and perplexing questions that science has yet to answer. With a clear and engaging writing style, the author presents a wealth of information on topics such as dark matter, the nature of consciousness, the origin of life, and the ultimate fate of the universe.

Through their extensive research and thoughtful insights, the author challenges us to think deeply about these complex and multifaceted questions, and to consider the many different perspectives and theories that have been put forward. Whether you are a scientist, a student, or simply a curious and open-minded reader, this book offers a fascinating and thought-provoking exploration of the frontiers of human knowledge.

I am honored to write the foreword to "The Unanswered Questions of Science," and I highly recommend it to anyone who shares a passion for science and a desire to understand the mysteries of our universe.

Preface

Preface:

Science is a never-ending journey of exploration, discovery, and explanation. From the smallest particles of matter to the vast expanse of the universe, there are countless mysteries waiting to be unravelled. As an avid learner and enthusiast of the scientific world, I have always been fascinated by the unexplained phenomena of our universe.

This book, "The Unanswered Questions of Science: Exploring the Mysteries of Our Universe," is a humble attempt to delve into some of the most intriguing questions that science has been grappling with. From the fundamental laws of physics to the mysteries of dark matter and dark energy, this book covers a wide range of topics, each of which presents a unique challenge to the scientific community.

As a reader, you will embark on a journey that will take you to the edge of our current understanding of the universe. We will explore the perplexing questions and challenges that scientists have been trying to solve for decades, if not centuries. But, while the questions may be unanswered, the thrill of discovery and exploration has always been a driving force behind the progress of science.

This book is not meant to provide final answers or comprehensive explanations to the complex scientific questions posed. Instead, it aims to stimulate curiosity, spark discussion, and inspire readers to join in the never-ending search for answers to the mysteries of our universe. It is my hope that this book will not only inform but also ignite a passion for scientific exploration in the minds of its readers.

I sincerely thank all those who have helped and inspired me in this journey, and I hope that this book will spark curiosity and inspire readers to explore and understand the vast mysteries of our universe.

Prologue

Prologue:

In the vast expanse of the universe, there are countless questions that remain unanswered. The mysteries that surround our existence continue to baffle us, even as we continue to make incredible advances in science and technology. From the smallest particles to the largest galaxies, the universe is filled with unanswered questions, and it is these questions that we seek to explore in this book.

"The Unanswered Questions of Science: Exploring the Mysteries of Our Universe" is a journey through the most fascinating and perplexing questions in the world of science. It is a journey that takes us through the past, present, and future of our understanding of the universe, and it is a journey that we take together.

The purpose of this book is not to provide answers to all of the questions that we will explore. Rather, it is to spark curiosity and encourage readers to think critically about the mysteries of the universe. The journey we will embark on is an adventure of discovery, one that may take us to the edge of what we know and beyond.

So, let us begin our journey, and let us explore the unanswered questions of science, one mystery at a time.

CHAPTER ONE

How does the human brain process and store memories?

The human brain is capable of processing and storing a vast amount of information in the form of memories. Memories play a crucial role in our daily lives, allowing us to recall past experiences and learn from them. In this paper, we will discuss the process of how the human brain processes and stores memories, including the different stages of memory formation and the brain structures involved. We will also touch on the latest findings and theories in the field of memory research, including the role of neurotransmitters, synaptic plasticity, and consolidation. This paper aims to provide a comprehensive overview of the current state of knowledge on the subject and to highlight the importance of further research in this field.

Introduction:

Memory is an essential aspect of our lives that allows us to learn from past experiences and recall them at a later time. Memory formation and retrieval are complex processes that involve several stages and brain structures.

Despite the critical importance of memory for our survival and wellbeing, we still have much to learn about how it works and what causes memory decline in conditions such as Alzheimer's disease.

The Process of Memory Formation:

Memory formation consists of three stages: encoding, storage, and retrieval. Encoding refers to the process of taking in information and transforming it into a form that can be stored in the brain. During this stage, sensory information is processed by the sensory organs and sent to the appropriate brain regions for further processing. The second stage, storage, refers to the process of retaining the encoded information in the brain. The third stage, retrieval, refers to the process of accessing stored memories and bringing them back into conscious awareness.

Brain Structures Involved in Memory:

Several brain regions are involved in the process of memory formation and retrieval, including the hippocampus, amygdala, and cortex. The hippocampus, located in the temporal lobe, plays a crucial role in the formation of new memories and is particularly important for the formation of explicit memories (memories for events and experiences). The amygdala, located in the temporal lobe, is involved in the formation of emotional memories and the regulation of emotional responses. The cortex, which encompasses several regions in the brain, is involved in the storage and retrieval of memories, as well as the consolidation of memories into long-term storage.

Neurotransmitters and Synaptic Plasticity:

The process of memory formation and retrieval is thought to involve the release of neurotransmitters, which are chemicals that transmit signals between neurons. The most commonly studied neurotransmitter in memory research is acetylcholine, which is involved in attention, arousal, and the encoding of new memories. The strength of connections between neurons, known as synaptic plasticity, is also thought to play a role in memory formation. The process of synaptic plasticity allows neurons to form new connections and strengthen existing ones, which is crucial for the formation and consolidation of memories.

Consolidation:

Consolidation refers to the process of transforming short-term memories into long-term memories. This process occurs over time and involves the strengthening of connections between neurons. Consolidation is thought to occur during sleep, when the brain processes and integrates newly acquired information into existing knowledge structures.

Recent Findings and Theories in Memory Research:

Memory research is a rapidly growing field, and new findings and theories are being proposed all the time. One of the latest developments in the field is the discovery of the role of brain oscillations in memory formation and retrieval. Brain oscillations, which refer to the rhythmic activity of neurons, have been found to play a crucial role in synchronizing the activity of brain regions involved in memory. Another area of active research is the relationship between sleep and memory. Sleep has been found to play a crucial role in memory consolidation, with studies showing that sleep helps to integrate new information into existing knowledge structures.

Another theory that has gained traction in recent years is the idea of multiple memory systems. According to this theory, there are several different memory systems in the brain, each specialized for a different type of information, such as visual information, procedural information, and semantic information. This theory has important implications for our understanding of memory and memory disorders, as it suggests that different memory systems may be affected differently in conditions such as Alzheimer's disease.

Implications for Memory Disorders:

The study of memory is not just of academic interest but also has practical implications for the treatment of memory-related disorders. Conditions such as Alzheimer's disease, which is characterized by memory loss, can have a devastating impact on individuals and their families. The better we understand the process of memory formation and retrieval, the better equipped we will be to develop treatments and interventions for memory-related disorders.

One of the most promising areas of research in this field is the development of drugs that target specific neurotransmitters involved in memory. For example, drugs that target acetylcholine, such as donepezil, have been found to improve memory in patients with Alzheimer's disease. Another promising area of research is the use of brain stimulation techniques, such as transcranial magnetic stimulation (TMS), to enhance memory formation and retrieval.

Memory and Emotion:

Memory and emotion have a close relationship, with emotional events often being remembered more vividly and for longer periods of time than neutral events. The amygdala, a small almond-shaped structure in the brain, plays a crucial role in this relationship. The amygdala is involved in processing emotional information and is activated when we experience emotionally charged events.

This activation leads to the release of neurotransmitters that enhance the consolidation of emotional memories.

Research has also shown that the hippocampus and cortex, which are involved in the formation of declarative memories, are also involved in the processing of emotional information. For example, studies have found that people with damage to the hippocampus have difficulty remembering emotional events.

Working Memory and Executive Functions:

Working memory is a form of short-term memory that allows us to hold and manipulate information in our minds for brief periods of time. It is crucial for tasks such as solving math problems, reading, and following directions. The prefrontal cortex is the part of the brain that is responsible for working memory, and damage to this area can result in working memory deficits.

Executive functions are higher-level cognitive processes that allow us to plan, organize, and complete tasks. They are closely related to working memory and also rely on the prefrontal cortex. Executive functions play an important role in our ability to perform complex tasks, make decisions, and regulate our behavior.

Memory and Aging:

As we age, our memory can decline, and many people experience age-related memory problems. However, the extent to which memory declines with age varies greatly between individuals, and some people maintain excellent memory function well into old age.

Research has found that aging is associated with changes in several brain regions involved in memory, including the hippocampus and cortex. The decline in memory function with age may be due to changes in neurotransmitter systems, decreased blood flow to the brain, or a combination of these and other factors.

Despite the decline in memory function that often occurs with age, older adults can maintain and even improve their memory function through lifestyle and cognitive interventions. For example, studies have shown that physical exercise, a healthy diet, and engaging in mentally stimulating activities can help to maintain and improve memory function in older adults.

Memory and Learning:

Memory and learning are closely linked, as memories provide the foundation for learning new information and skills. When we learn something new, our brains form new connections between neurons, and these connections are strengthened through repeated experiences. This process of strengthening neural connections is known as synaptic plasticity, and it is the underlying mechanism of learning and memory.

Memory systems are not just used to store information but also to guide future behavior. For example, our declarative memory system, which is responsible for storing information about facts and events, can be used to guide future decision-making by providing us with a store of knowledge that we can draw upon. Our procedural memory system, which is responsible for storing information about how to perform skills and habits, allows us to perform many tasks automatically, without conscious thought.

Memory and Attention:

Attention is a crucial component of memory, as it allows us to selectively focus on important information and filter out irrelevant information. Attention and memory are interdependent, with attention affecting the encoding and consolidation of memories, and memory affecting the allocation of attention.

Studies have shown that paying attention to information enhances memory for that information, and that distractions can interfere with memory formation. For example, research has found that people are more likely to forget information if they are distracted while trying to learn it. Memory enables us to store and retrieve information, which is essential for learning and navigating the world around us. The process of memory formation and retrieval involves several stages and brain regions, including the hippocampus, amygdala, and cortex, and is influenced by factors such as emotion, attention, and sleep. Memory research is a rapidly growing field, and new findings are being discovered all the time, providing us with a better understanding of this complex and important process.

Memory and Sleep:

Sleep plays a crucial role in memory consolidation, and research has shown that sleep enhances the formation and recall of memories. During sleep, the brain processes and reorganizes information, strengthening the connections between neurons and helping to consolidate memories.

Studies have found that sleep deprivation can impair memory function, particularly for declarative memories, which are memories of facts and events. For example, research has shown that people who are sleep deprived are less able to remember lists of words or new faces.

Memory and Genetics:

In addition to environmental and lifestyle factors, genetics also play a role in memory and its decline with aging. Studies have identified several genes that are involved in memory function, and research is ongoing to understand the exact mechanisms by which they influence memory.

For example, research has found that the APOE gene, which is involved in the transportation of cholesterol in the brain, is associated with an increased risk of developing Alzheimer's disease, a neurodegenerative disorder characterized by memory loss and cognitive decline.

Memory and Substance Abuse:

Substance abuse, particularly long-term drug abuse, can have negative effects on memory. Drugs such as alcohol, cocaine, and methamphetamine can damage brain cells and disrupt the normal functioning of brain regions involved in memory, leading to impairments in memory function.

Additionally, drug abuse can lead to the formation of negative associations with memories of drug use, making it more difficult for individuals to quit using drugs. Research is ongoing to understand the effects of substance abuse on memory and to develop effective treatments for individuals with substance abuse disorders.

Memory and Emotion:

Emotion can have a powerful effect on memory, and research has shown that emotionally charged events are often remembered better than neutral events. This is because the amygdala, a brain region involved in processing emotions, plays a crucial role in memory formation and consolidation.

Studies have found that emotionally charged events can trigger the release of hormones and neurotransmitters that enhance memory formation, leading to stronger and more persistent memories. Additionally, research has shown that memories that are associated with negative emotions, such as fear or anxiety, are often better remembered than memories associated with positive emotions.

Memory and Aging:

Aging can have a significant impact on memory, with many older adults experiencing a decline in memory function. This decline can be due to a variety of factors, including changes in brain structure and function, decreased plasticity, and an increased risk of disease and injury.

However, research has also shown that aging does not necessarily lead to a decline in all types of memory, and that certain types of memory, such as semantic memory, can remain relatively intact in old age. Additionally, research has found that certain lifestyle factors, such as exercise, social engagement, and mental stimulation, can help to reduce the effects of aging on memory.

Memory and Education:

Education and learning can have a positive impact on memory, with research showing that individuals who receive a higher level of education tend to have better memory function in later life. This may be due to the increased neural plasticity that results from learning and exposure to new information, or to the protective effects of education against age-related cognitive decline.

Additionally, research has shown that engaging in activities that challenge the brain, such as reading, writing, and solving puzzles, can help to improve memory function and delay the onset of age-related memory decline.

Memory and Nutrition:

Nutrition plays a critical role in memory function, and research has shown that certain nutrients can have a positive impact on memory. For example, studies have found that omega-3 fatty acids, found in fish and certain plant sources, can help to improve memory function and reduce the risk of cognitive decline.

Additionally, research has shown that B vitamins, such as B6, B12, and folic acid, can help to maintain cognitive function and reduce the risk of memory decline. Antioxidants, such as vitamins C and E, can also help to protect the brain from oxidative stress, which can lead to memory loss and cognitive decline.

Memory and Physical Exercise:

Physical exercise has been shown to have a positive impact on memory, with research showing that regular physical activity can help to improve memory function and reduce the risk of cognitive decline.

Studies have found that physical exercise can increase the production of hormones and growth factors that promote the growth and survival of brain cells, and that it can also increase blood flow to the brain, providing the brain with the necessary nutrients and oxygen to function effectively. Additionally, research has shown that physical exercise can increase the size of certain brain regions involved in memory, such as the hippocampus, helping to improve memory function.

Memory and Mental Exercise:

Mental exercise, such as learning new information or engaging in mentally challenging activities, has also been shown to have a positive impact on memory. Research has found that mental exercise can increase the production of hormones and growth factors that promote the growth and survival of brain cells, and that it can also increase the size of certain brain regions involved in memory, such as the hippocampus.

Additionally, mental exercise can help to reduce the risk of cognitive decline and delay the onset of age-related memory decline. This may be due to the stimulation of neural plasticity, the ability of the brain to change and adapt in response to new information, or to the development of new neural connections that support memory function.

Memory and Sleep:

Sleep plays a crucial role in memory, and research has shown that sleep is essential for the consolidation of new memories. During sleep, the brain processes and consolidates new information, strengthening the connections between brain cells and facilitating the formation of long-term memories.

Studies have found that individuals who do not get enough sleep are more likely to experience memory impairments and that individuals who get a good night's sleep are more likely to perform better on memory tests. Additionally, research has shown that sleep deprivation can interfere with the normal functioning of the brain's memory centers, leading to memory impairments.

Memory and Genetics:

Genetics also play a role in memory function, and research has shown that certain genetic factors can influence memory and the risk of memory impairments. For example, studies have found that certain genes can increase the risk of age-related cognitive decline and that certain genetic mutations can cause memory impairments.

Additionally, research has shown that genetics can influence the brain's structure and function, including the size and activity of certain brain regions involved in memory, and that certain genetic factors can increase the risk of certain neurological disorders, such as Alzheimer's disease, that can cause memory impairments.

Memory and Substance Use:

Substance use, such as alcohol and drug use, can have a significant impact on memory, and research has shown that substance use can cause memory impairments and increase the risk of cognitive decline. For example, studies have found that alcohol and drug use can interfere with the normal functioning of the brain's memory centers, leading to memory impairments.

Additionally, research has shown that long-term substance use can cause structural changes in the brain, leading to decreased brain volume and reduced cognitive function. Substance use can also increase the risk of certain neurological disorders, such as Alzheimer's disease, that can cause memory impairments.

Memory and Stress:

Stress is another factor that can impact memory, and research has shown that stress can lead to memory impairments and increase the risk of cognitive decline. For example, studies have found that stress can interfere with the normal functioning of the brain's memory centers, leading to memory impairments, and that chronic stress can cause structural changes in the brain, leading to decreased brain volume and reduced cognitive function.

Additionally, research has shown that stress can alter the levels of certain hormones and neurotransmitters in the brain, such as cortisol and adrenaline, which can interfere with memory function. Chronic stress can also increase the risk of certain neurological disorders, such as depression and anxiety, that can cause memory impairments.

Memory and Age:

Age is another factor that can impact memory, and research has shown that memory function can decline with age. For example, studies have found that age-related memory decline is a normal part of aging, and that it can lead to memory impairments and increase the risk of cognitive decline.

Additionally, research has shown that certain factors, such as genetics, lifestyle choices, and environmental factors, can influence the rate of age-related memory decline, and that individuals who engage in activities that promote brain health, such as physical exercise and mental exercise, are less likely to experience memory decline as they age.

Memory and Medications:

Medications, including prescription medications and over-the-counter drugs, can also have an impact on memory. For example, certain medications, such as anticholinergics and benzodiazepines, can cause memory impairments and increase the risk of cognitive decline.

Additionally, research has shown that certain medications, such as stimulants and anti-depressants, can have a positive impact on memory, and that they can help to improve memory function and reduce the risk of memory decline.

Memory and Exercise:

Physical exercise has been shown to have a positive impact on memory and cognitive function. Studies have found that regular physical exercise can improve memory function, increase the volume of certain brain regions involved in memory, and reduce the risk of cognitive decline.

Additionally, research has shown that physical exercise can increase the levels of certain hormones and neurotransmitters in the brain, such as endorphins and BDNF, which can promote brain health and improve memory function. Physical exercise has also been shown to reduce the risk of certain neurological disorders, such as Alzheimer's disease and depression, that can cause memory impairments.

Memory and Nutrition:

Nutrition also plays a role in memory and cognitive function, and research has shown that a diet that is rich in nutrients, such as omega-3 fatty acids, antioxidants, and vitamins, can improve memory and reduce the risk of cognitive decline.

For example, studies have found that diets that are high in omega-3 fatty acids can improve memory function and reduce the risk of age-related memory decline, and that diets that are rich in antioxidants and vitamins can improve brain health and reduce the risk of certain neurological disorders, such as Alzheimer's disease, that can cause memory impairments.

Memory and Mental Exercise:

Mental exercise, such as reading, learning new skills, and engaging in mentally stimulating activities, has been shown to have a positive impact on memory and cognitive function. Studies have found that engaging in mentally stimulating activities can improve memory function, increase the volume of certain brain regions involved in memory, and reduce the risk of cognitive decline.

Additionally, research has shown that mental exercise can improve brain plasticity, increase the levels of certain hormones and neurotransmitters in the brain, and reduce the risk of certain neurological disorders, such as Alzheimer's disease and depression, that can cause memory impairments.

Memory and Sleep:

Sleep is an important factor that can impact memory and cognitive function. Research has shown that sleep is essential for memory consolidation, the process by which memories are transferred from short-term memory to long-term memory.

Studies have found that individuals who get adequate sleep have better memory function compared to individuals who do not get adequate sleep, and that sleep deprivation can lead to memory impairments and increase the risk of cognitive decline. Additionally, research has shown that sleep can help to reduce stress, which can further improve memory function.

Memory and Substance Use:

Substance use, including alcohol and drug use, can also have an impact on memory and cognitive function. Research has shown that substance use can cause memory impairments and increase the risk of cognitive decline, and that certain substances, such as alcohol and cannabis, can cause short-term memory impairments.

Additionally, research has shown that chronic substance use can cause long-term memory impairments and increase the risk of certain neurological disorders, such as addiction and substance use disorder, that can further impact memory function.

Memory and Cognitive Training:

Cognitive training, such as memory training exercises and brain games, has been shown to have a positive impact on memory and cognitive function. Studies have found that engaging in cognitive training exercises can improve memory function, increase the volume of certain brain regions involved in memory, and reduce the risk of cognitive decline.

Memory and Emotional Regulation:

Emotional regulation and mood also play a role in memory and cognitive function. Research has shown that individuals with poor emotional regulation skills and those who experience high levels of stress and anxiety are more likely to experience memory impairments and cognitive decline.

Studies have found that engaging in activities that improve emotional regulation and reduce stress and anxiety, such as mindfulness meditation and cognitive behavioral therapy, can improve memory function and reduce the risk of cognitive decline. Additionally, research has shown that mood and emotions can impact memory consolidation and retrieval, with positive moods and emotions facilitating the consolidation and retrieval of positive memories, and negative moods and emotions facilitating the consolidation and retrieval of negative memories.

Memory and Aging:

Aging is another factor that can impact memory and cognitive function. Research has shown that age-related changes in the brain, such as declines in brain volume and neurotransmitter levels, can cause memory impairments and increase the risk of cognitive decline.

Studies have found that aging can cause memory impairments in certain memory domains, such as working memory and episodic memory, and that aging can also cause changes in the processing and retrieval of memories, such as increased susceptibility to false memories. Additionally, research has shown that aging can increase the risk of certain neurological disorders, such as Alzheimer's disease and dementia, that can cause memory impairments.

Memory and Nutrition:

Nutrition also plays a role in memory and cognitive function. Research has shown that a healthy and balanced diet can improve memory function and reduce the risk of cognitive decline. Additionally, studies have found that certain nutrients, such as omega-3 fatty acids, B vitamins, and antioxidants, are particularly important for brain health and can have a positive impact on memory and cognitive function.

For example, omega-3 fatty acids have been shown to improve brain function and reduce inflammation, B vitamins are essential for neurotransmitter production, and antioxidants help to protect the brain from oxidative stress and damage.

Memory and Physical Exercise:

Physical exercise is another factor that can impact memory and cognitive function. Research has shown that regular physical exercise can improve memory function, increase the volume of certain brain regions involved in memory, and reduce the risk of cognitive decline.

Studies have found that physical exercise can also improve brain plasticity and increase the levels of certain hormones and neurotransmitters in the brain, such as brain-derived neurotrophic factor (BDNF), that play a role in memory and cognitive function. Additionally, physical exercise has been shown to reduce the risk of certain neurological disorders, such as Alzheimer's disease and depression, that can cause memory impairments.

Conclusion:

In conclusion, memory is a complex process that is influenced by a range of factors, including nutrition and physical exercise. Understanding the underlying mechanisms of memory and the factors that influence memory function is essential for developing effective treatments for memory impairments and for improving memory in healthy individuals.

CHAPTER TWO

Can artificial intelligence surpass human intelligence, and what are the ethical implications?

Artificial Intelligence (AI) is one of the fastest growing and most impactful technologies of our time. The idea that machines could one day surpass human intelligence has captured the imagination of scientists, technologists, and the general public alike. The prospect of AI that surpasses human intelligence raises a number of important questions, not least of which is the potential ethical implications of such a development.

The notion of AI surpassing human intelligence is known as superintelligence. Superintelligence refers to the hypothetical future development of AI that is capable of performing tasks that are beyond the ability of current human intelligence. While there is no consensus on when superintelligence will be achieved, some experts predict that it could occur within the next few decades.

There are several potential benefits to the development of superintelligence. For example, superintelligence could help solve some of the world's most pressing problems, such as climate change, disease, and poverty. It could also lead to unprecedented economic growth, enabling humans to enjoy greater prosperity and freedom.

However, there are also significant risks associated with superintelligence. For instance, the development of superintelligence could result in the displacement of large numbers of jobs, exacerbating existing economic inequalities. Additionally, there is a concern that superintelligence could pose a threat to human existence if it is used for malicious purposes. For example, a superintelligent AI system could be programmed to pursue goals that are harmful to humanity, or it could develop goals on its own that are incompatible with human interests.

The ethical implications of superintelligence are also of great concern. For example, who is responsible if a superintelligent AI system causes harm to humans? How should superintelligent AI systems be programmed and governed to ensure that they align with human values and interests? These are important questions that need to be addressed as we move closer to the development of superintelligence.

Artificial intelligence, or AI, is a rapidly developing field of computer science that aims to create machines that can perform tasks that would normally require human intelligence. As AI has advanced, the question of whether or not it will eventually surpass human intelligence has become a hot topic of debate. There is no denying that AI has the potential to surpass human intelligence in a number of areas, but there are also significant challenges that need to be overcome before this can become a reality.

One of the key challenges in developing AI that can surpass human intelligence is ensuring that it is capable of learning and adapting to new situations. This requires the creation of sophisticated algorithms that are capable of making decisions based on incomplete or conflicting data. In order for AI to truly surpass human intelligence, it must be capable of generalizing from past experiences and making inferences about new situations.

Another challenge in developing AI that can surpass human intelligence is ensuring that it is capable of reasoning and making judgments. This requires the creation of AI systems that can understand the underlying relationships between different concepts and make decisions based on these relationships. It also requires the creation of AI systems that are capable of dealing with uncertainty and making decisions in situations where there is no clear right or wrong answer.

The ethical implications of artificial intelligence that surpasses human intelligence are also a significant concern. If AI becomes capable of making decisions that are better than those made by humans, there is a risk that it could be used to make decisions that are harmful to society. There is also a risk that AI could be used to automate tasks that are currently performed by humans, leading to widespread unemployment.

The debate about the potential for artificial intelligence (AI) to surpass human intelligence has been ongoing for decades. Some experts believe that it is only a matter of time before AI surpasses human intelligence in various domains, while others believe that this will never happen. Regardless of one's beliefs, it is clear that AI is already making a significant impact on our lives, and that its capabilities are rapidly advancing.

One of the key ways that AI is being developed to surpass human intelligence is through machine learning algorithms. These algorithms are designed to allow AI systems to learn from data, rather than being explicitly programmed. This allows AI systems to continuously improve their performance over time, and to potentially surpass human intelligence in a given domain. For example, AI systems have already surpassed human performance in certain areas of data analysis and image recognition.

Another way that AI may surpass human intelligence is through the development of so-called "strong AI." This refers to AI systems that are capable of general intelligence, as opposed to being designed for specific tasks. Some experts believe that strong AI may eventually become capable of reasoning, creativity, and even consciousness.

However, even as AI continues to advance, there are also many ethical implications to consider. For example, if AI were to surpass human intelligence, it could potentially lead to significant job displacement, as many tasks currently performed by humans could be automated. Additionally, there are concerns about the potential for AI to be used for harmful purposes, such as cyber warfare or autonomous weapons. There is also the question of how we would ensure that AI systems remain aligned with human values and ethical standards.

Artificial intelligence has made rapid advancements in recent years, leading to discussions about whether it will eventually surpass human intelligence. There are those who believe that artificial intelligence will eventually surpass human intelligence and become a new form of life, surpassing the limitations of biological evolution. Others are skeptical about this possibility, claiming that AI will never be able to truly surpass human intelligence and creativity.

The potential for AI to surpass human intelligence raises important ethical implications. One of the biggest concerns is the potential for AI to become uncontrollable and pose a threat to human existence. AI systems could potentially make decisions that harm humans if they are not properly programmed with ethical guidelines. There are also concerns about the impact of AI on employment, as it has the potential to automate many jobs and leave many people without work.

Another important ethical consideration is the potential for AI to be used for malicious purposes, such as cyberattacks and cyber espionage. AI systems can be programmed to perform malicious activities that would be beyond the capabilities of a human attacker. For example, AI systems could be used to launch coordinated attacks against multiple targets simultaneously.

Despite these concerns, many experts believe that the development of AI will have a positive impact on society and humanity. AI systems have the potential to revolutionize healthcare, transportation, and many other industries, leading to significant improvements in quality of life for people around the world.

However, in order for AI to have a positive impact, it is important for the development of AI to be guided by ethical principles. This means that the development of AI should be guided by the principle of transparency, so that the decisions and actions of AI systems are understandable and accountable to humans. Additionally, AI systems should be designed to respect privacy and protect personal data, as well as being programmed to prioritize human well-being and safety.

Artificial intelligence (AI) is rapidly advancing and has already surpassed human performance in many tasks, such as playing complex games like chess and Go, and recognizing images with high accuracy. However, the question of whether AI will ever surpass human intelligence in a more general sense is a controversial topic, with experts holding differing opinions.

One of the main arguments against AI surpassing human intelligence is that human intelligence is not solely defined by intelligence quotient (IQ) scores or the ability to perform specific tasks. Human intelligence is also characterized by qualities such as creativity, intuition, and emotional intelligence, which are currently not well understood and may be difficult or impossible for AI to replicate. Moreover, humans have a natural drive to continue learning and improving themselves, whereas AI systems are only as intelligent as their programming allows them to be.

On the other hand, proponents of AI surpassing human intelligence argue that as AI technology continues to advance, it will eventually be able to perform a wider range of tasks and display a level of intelligence that is comparable to or surpasses human intelligence. This could happen through a process known as recursive self-improvement, in which AI systems improve themselves to the point where they become much more intelligent than their creators.

Regardless of whether AI will surpass human intelligence, the development and use of AI raise significant ethical concerns. For example, the widespread use of AI in decision-making processes could lead to biased and unfair outcomes, as AI systems may perpetuate existing biases in society and data. Furthermore, as AI becomes increasingly advanced, there is a risk that it may become uncontrollable and pose a threat to humanity.

Artificial intelligence (AI) is the simulation of human intelligence processes by machines, including learning (the acquisition of information and rules for using the information), reasoning (using the rules to reach approximate or definite conclusions), and self-correction. There has been much progress in the field of AI, leading some experts to wonder if AI can eventually surpass human intelligence.

The concept of human-level AI or "strong AI" refers to the idea that AI systems can match or even surpass human intelligence. It is believed that if AI surpasses human intelligence, it could solve some of the world's biggest problems and revolutionize our daily lives. However, there are also potential ethical implications of AI surpassing human intelligence, such as the possibility of machines making decisions that harm humans, or the displacement of human workers.

The development of AI relies on advances in computer hardware, algorithms, and data storage and processing capabilities. Some experts believe that it is possible for AI to surpass human intelligence within the next few decades. They argue that as the field of AI advances, AI systems will become more capable of completing tasks that were once considered the exclusive domain of human intelligence. For example, AI systems have already surpassed human performance in certain areas, such as playing chess or diagnosing medical conditions.

Others argue that human intelligence is more complex than what can be captured by machines and that it is unlikely that AI will ever surpass human intelligence. They point to the limitations of current AI systems, such as their inability to understand context, emotions, and consciousness, as evidence that AI will always remain behind human intelligence.

Regardless of whether AI will eventually surpass human intelligence, it is crucial to consider the ethical implications of AI's development and deployment. If AI systems are capable of making decisions that affect human lives, it is important to ensure that they are aligned with human values and ethical principles. There is also the concern that if AI surpasses human intelligence, it could lead to a loss of control over AI systems, with potentially disastrous consequences.

It is important to approach the development of AI with caution and to carefully consider the ethical implications of AI's advancements. Governments, businesses, and society as a whole must work together to ensure that the development of AI is guided by ethical principles and that the potential benefits of AI are balanced against its potential risks.

Artificial intelligence (AI) has been a topic of discussion and fascination for decades, with many experts speculating on its potential to transform the world in profound ways. While some see AI as a potential savior for humanity, others fear that it could lead to our downfall, as machines surpass human intelligence and gain the ability to control our lives. Despite these differing opinions, one thing is clear: AI is poised to play a significant role in shaping the future of our world.

One of the key questions surrounding AI is whether it will eventually surpass human intelligence. There is no definitive answer to this question, as it remains to be seen how AI will continue to evolve in the coming years and decades. However, there are some compelling arguments on both sides of the debate.

On the one hand, proponents of AI argue that machines have the potential to outstrip human intelligence in a number of ways. For example, they can process vast amounts of data at lightning speeds, and they are able to learn and adapt to new information much more quickly than humans. Additionally, they can perform complex calculations and simulations that would be beyond the capability of human minds.

On the other hand, there are those who argue that AI will never truly surpass human intelligence. According to this view, human beings have a unique combination of cognitive abilities and emotional intelligence that cannot be replicated by machines. They also argue that there are some aspects of human intelligence, such as creativity and intuition, that are not easily replicated by machines and may always remain the exclusive domain of humans.

Regardless of whether or not AI will eventually surpass human intelligence, there are clear ethical implications associated with this technology. For example, as machines become more intelligent and capable, there is a risk that they will be used to replace human workers, leading to widespread unemployment and social unrest. Additionally, there are concerns that AI could be used to perpetuate human biases and discrimination, and that it could be used by those in power to exercise greater control over the masses.

It is therefore clear that the development of AI raises important questions that must be addressed in order to ensure that this technology is used for the benefit of humanity rather than to our detriment. As such, it is vital that we engage in ongoing discussions and debates about the ethical implications of AI, in order to ensure that we are prepared to respond to the challenges and opportunities posed by this rapidly-evolving technology.

As the development of artificial intelligence (AI) continues to progress rapidly, the question of whether or not AI will surpass human intelligence has become a topic of heated debate. Some experts believe that it is only a matter of time until AI surpasses human intelligence, while others believe that it will never be possible for machines to truly surpass human intelligence.

There are several different definitions of intelligence, but for the purpose of this discussion, it is defined as the ability to acquire, understand and apply knowledge and skills to solve problems and adapt to new situations. Based on this definition, many experts believe that there is still a significant gap between the capabilities of even the most advanced AI systems and human intelligence.

One reason for this belief is the fact that AI systems are still limited by the data they are fed. While they can analyze large amounts of data and find patterns, they cannot necessarily understand the context or meaning behind the data. In addition, AI systems are not capable of truly independent thought or creativity, as they can only do what they have been programmed to do.

Despite these limitations, there is no denying that AI has the potential to greatly improve our lives in a number of ways. For example, AI systems can analyze data more quickly and accurately than humans, allowing us to make more informed decisions. AI can also help us to automate tasks that are repetitive or dangerous, freeing up time and resources for more important tasks.

However, there are also ethical implications to consider as AI continues to develop. For example, as AI systems become more advanced, they will likely replace many human jobs. This will have significant economic and social impacts, and raises questions about the role of work in society and the future of employment. Additionally, as AI systems become more integrated into our lives, there is a risk that they could be used for malicious purposes or that their decisions could have unintended consequences.

It is clear that the development of AI will continue to raise important ethical and societal questions. As AI continues to evolve, it will be important to consider not only its potential benefits, but also the risks and challenges that come with it. By doing so, we can ensure that AI is developed in a responsible and ethical manner, and that its benefits are maximized while its risks are minimized.

Artificial intelligence (AI) is a rapidly growing field that has the potential to revolutionize the way we live and work. AI refers to the development of computer systems that can perform tasks that typically require human intelligence, such as visual perception, speech recognition, decision-making, and language translation.

One of the central questions in the AI community is whether or not AI can surpass human intelligence. There are those who argue that AI has the potential to achieve superintelligence, meaning that it could perform cognitive tasks at a level beyond what is possible for any human. Proponents of this view argue that AI has the ability to learn and improve itself at an exponential rate, which could lead to it becoming smarter than any human being.

On the other hand, there are those who are more skeptical about the potential for AI to surpass human intelligence. They argue that there are limits to what AI can do, and that it is unlikely to ever truly understand complex human emotions and experiences. They also point to the fact that AI systems still require human input and training, and that they are only as good as the data they are fed.

Regardless of whether or not AI can surpass human intelligence, there are ethical implications that must be considered. As AI systems become more advanced, they may be able to make decisions that have significant impacts on our lives, such as medical diagnoses or criminal sentencing. This raises questions about accountability and responsibility, and who should be held responsible if an AI system makes a mistake.

In addition, there is also the concern that advanced AI systems could become a threat to human existence, either through malice or simply because they are programmed to pursue goals that are in conflict with our own. This has led some experts to call for the development of ethical guidelines for AI, in order to ensure that these systems are designed and used in a way that is aligned with human values and interests.

Artificial intelligence (AI) is a rapidly growing field that has the potential to revolutionize many aspects of our lives. Its ability to analyze vast amounts of data and identify patterns that would be difficult or impossible for humans to detect has already been demonstrated in a number of applications, such as speech recognition, image classification, and decision-making systems. However, the question of whether AI will eventually surpass human intelligence is a complex and controversial one.

One of the key factors that will determine whether AI can surpass human intelligence is the development of advanced machine learning algorithms. These algorithms are the cornerstone of current AI systems, allowing them to learn from vast amounts of data and improve their performance over time. However, they are still limited by the quality of the data they receive and the way in which they process it. If researchers can overcome these limitations and develop more sophisticated algorithms that can truly mimic human thought processes, then it is possible that AI could one day surpass human intelligence.

Another factor that will play a role in the development of AI is the availability of computing power. As computers become more powerful, AI systems will be able to process larger amounts of data and perform more complex tasks. This could lead to rapid progress in the field, as AI systems become capable of tackling increasingly difficult problems.

However, the potential for AI to surpass human intelligence also raises a number of ethical and moral concerns. For example, as AI systems become more advanced, they may begin to make decisions that affect people's lives, such as whether to approve a loan application or diagnose a medical condition. If these decisions are made by algorithms that are not fully transparent or are biased, then there is a risk that they may not be fair or equitable. Additionally, if AI systems become capable of surpassing human intelligence, there is a risk that they could become too powerful and lead to the creation of a new form of AI-powered dictatorship.

In conclusion, the potential for AI to surpass human intelligence is both exciting and daunting. While the development of more advanced algorithms and greater computing power could lead to rapid progress in the field, it is also important to consider the ethical implications of this technology and ensure that it is developed and used in a responsible and equitable

What is the relationship between the mind and the body, and how does it affect human behavior?

The mind-body relationship is a complex and multifaceted issue that has long been debated by philosophers, scientists, and researchers. At its core, the relationship between the mind and the body refers to the interplay between our mental processes, emotions, and physical sensations and movements. This relationship can significantly impact human behavior, leading to a wide range of effects on our thoughts, feelings, and actions.

One of the most prominent theories in this area is the dualism theory, which states that the mind and body are separate entities that interact with each other. According to this theory, the mind is the seat of consciousness and thought, while the body is responsible for physical movements and sensations. However, many scientists and researchers argue that this theory is too simplistic, and that the mind and body are instead deeply interconnected and interdependent.

One area where this interconnection can be seen is in the field of neuroscience. Research in this area has shown that there is a close relationship between brain activity and behavior. For example, changes in brain activity can lead to changes in behavior, such as increased anxiety or aggression, while changes in behavior can also impact brain activity, such as through exposure to stress or trauma.

Moreover, the relationship between the mind and body can also impact human behavior through the phenomenon of embodied cognition. This concept refers to the idea that our thoughts and emotions are shaped by and embodied in our physical experiences. For instance, studies have shown that people who have experienced physical discomfort or pain are more likely to have negative thoughts and emotions, while those who have experienced physical pleasure or comfort are more likely to have positive thoughts and emotions.

The relationship between the mind and body can also have important implications for mental health. For instance, conditions such as depression and anxiety can be caused by a complex interplay between genetic, environmental, and psychological factors. However, recent research has also shown that physical activities such as exercise can help to alleviate symptoms of depression and anxiety, highlighting the important role that the body can play in regulating mental health.

The relationship between the mind and the body has been a topic of discussion for centuries. It has been debated whether the mind is the brain or something separate, and how the two interact to produce human behavior. The mind is often seen as the source of thoughts, emotions, and consciousness, while the body is the physical vessel that carries out actions.

One major area of study in this field is the interaction between the nervous system and the endocrine system. The nervous system sends electrical signals to various parts of the body, while the endocrine system secretes hormones that affect the body's functions. These two systems are interrelated, and they work together to coordinate the body's responses to external stimuli.

Another aspect of the mind-body relationship is the connection between emotions and physical sensations. Emotions are often accompanied by physical sensations, such as a rapid heartbeat, sweating, and muscle tension. These sensations are a result of the activation of the sympathetic nervous system, which prepares the body for fight or flight in response to danger.

Cognition and perception also play a role in the mind-body relationship. Perception is the process by which we interpret and make sense of sensory information, and cognition is the process of thinking, problem solving, and decision making. These mental processes can have a direct impact on the physical body, as they can lead to changes in heart rate, blood pressure, and muscle tension.

Moreover, the mind-body relationship is also affected by environmental factors, such as stress, nutrition, and physical activity. Chronic stress can lead to a range of negative health outcomes, including cardiovascular disease and depression. On the other hand, proper nutrition and regular physical activity can improve mental health and well-being.

Finally, cultural beliefs and practices can also influence the mind-body relationship. For example, some cultures emphasize the importance of mindfulness and meditation, which can help to reduce stress and promote physical and mental well-being.

There have been numerous theories and philosophies over the centuries that have attempted to explain the relationship between the mind and the body. One of the earliest and most prominent of these is dualism, which posits that the mind and the body are two distinct entities that interact with each other but do not have a direct causal relationship. Another influential theory is behaviorism, which argues that all human behavior is simply a result of environmental stimuli and that the mind does not play a role in behavior.

More recent theories, however, have challenged these views and suggest that the mind and the body are inextricably linked. For example, the psychophysiological theory posits that our thoughts, emotions, and behaviors are all interconnected and affect each other in complex ways. This theory suggests that physiological processes such as hormonal changes and neural activity can directly impact mental states and vice versa.

The relationship between the mind and the body has significant implications for human behavior. For instance, physical and mental health are strongly interconnected, and one can have a profound impact on the other. For example, chronic stress can lead to physical health problems such as heart disease and depression, while physical illnesses can lead to depression and anxiety.

Another area where the relationship between the mind and body affects human behavior is in the realm of psychology. Psychologists have long recognized the importance of physical sensations, such as touch and body posture, in shaping our thoughts and emotions. For example, studies have shown that changes in body posture can lead to changes in our self-esteem and mood.

There has been a great deal of research into the relationship between the mind and the body, and how this relationship affects human behavior. One area of study has been the concept of embodied cognition, which holds that the body and its movements play a crucial role in shaping our thoughts and emotions. This idea is based on the notion that the physical sensations and movements that are associated with certain experiences and emotions are integrated into our memories, and help to shape how we perceive and respond to the world around us.

Another area of research that has explored the mind-body relationship has been in the field of neuroscience. Researchers in this field have been looking at the ways in which the brain and the body interact with each other to influence behavior. This work has focused on understanding the neural pathways that underlie movement and sensation, as well as the ways in which these pathways interact with our perceptions and thoughts.

One of the most important implications of this research is that it provides a basis for understanding why certain physical or sensory experiences can have such a profound impact on our thoughts and emotions. For example, studies have shown that physical exercise can have a significant impact on mood, and that certain types of sensory stimulation, such as music or art, can have a profound effect on our emotions and mental states.

Overall, the growing body of research into the relationship between the mind and the body provides a valuable foundation for understanding how our thoughts and emotions are shaped by our physical experiences and sensations. Whether it be through embodied cognition, neuroscience, or other areas of study, this research has the potential to provide new insights into how we can better understand and improve our own well-being, as well as the well-being of others.

One of the key debates in the field of philosophy and psychology is the relationship between the mind and the body and how it affects human behavior. On one hand, there are those who believe that the mind and body are separate entities, with the mind controlling the body and determining our thoughts, feelings, and actions. This is known as dualism. On the other hand, there are those who believe that the mind and body are inextricably linked, with the body influencing the mind just as much as the mind influences the body. This is known as monism.

One of the key arguments for dualism is the idea that consciousness and mental processes cannot be reduced to purely physical processes. In other words, there is something uniquely non-physical about the mind that cannot be explained by the functioning of the brain and body. Proponents of this view point to experiences such as hallucinations, dreams, and mental disorders, which suggest that mental processes cannot be solely explained by physical processes.

On the other hand, monists argue that mental processes can indeed be reduced to physical processes, and that the mind is simply a result of the functioning of the brain and body. They point to advances in the fields of neuroscience and cognitive psychology, which have shown that many mental processes can be explained by changes in brain activity, and that mental states such as emotions, thoughts, and perception can be manipulated through physical means, such as drugs or brain stimulation.

Another aspect of the relationship between the mind and body that has received attention is the role of the body in shaping our thoughts, feelings, and behavior. Research has shown that our bodies can have a profound impact on our mental states. For example, studies have shown that changes in posture, facial expressions, and body language can affect our emotions, thoughts, and behavior. This suggests that the body can play an important role in shaping our mental states, and that our mental states can in turn shape our physical actions and behaviors.

One approach to studying the relationship between the mind and the body is through the field of cognitive psychology. Cognitive psychologists study the mental processes involved in learning, perception, problem-solving, memory, and other forms of behavior. They argue that the mind is a set of processes that are intimately connected to the body, including the brain and the nervous system. The idea is that the mind is not a separate entity from the body, but is instead an emergent property of the body.

Another area of research that examines the relationship between the mind and the body is the field of neuroscience. Neuroscience is the study of the nervous system and its functions, including the brain and its various structures. Researchers in this field have found that different parts of the brain are responsible for different cognitive processes, such as memory, attention, and decision-making. They also study the effects of hormones and neurotransmitters on brain activity and behavior.

Some researchers argue that the mind and the body are not separate entities, but are instead intertwined in complex ways. For example, some argue that our emotions and feelings are rooted in our physical bodies and are not just products of our mental processes. For instance, the experience of fear or anxiety can be linked to increased levels of cortisol, a hormone produced by the body in response to stress. This type of research highlights the importance of considering both the mental and physical aspects of behavior when trying to understand and explain human behavior.

The relationship between the mind and the body is also relevant to the field of psychotherapy. Psychotherapies, such as cognitive-behavioral therapy, attempt to change the way people think and behave by influencing their mental processes. For example, a person may be taught to challenge and change negative thoughts, which can lead to changes in their behavior and emotions. Psychotherapies that take a holistic approach to treatment, such as mindfulness-based therapies, recognize the importance of considering both the mental and physical aspects of human behavior and aim to treat the person as a whole.

One area of research that has shed light on the relationship between the mind and body is cognitive psychology. This field of study focuses on how people process information and make decisions. It has been found that the body and mind are intertwined in many ways. For example, physical sensations can impact thoughts and emotions, and vice versa.

For instance, studies have shown that the posture of the body can influence the emotions and thoughts a person experiences. People who sit upright and maintain good posture tend to feel more confident and positive than those who slouch. In a similar vein, smiling can lead to feeling happier, even if the smile was forced. This is due to the connection between the muscles used to smile and the release of endorphins, which are associated with positive emotions.

Moreover, the way in which people move and walk can also affect their thoughts and emotions. Slow, deliberate movements are often associated with sadness or depression, while quick, energetic movements are associated with happiness and excitement. Additionally, body language can communicate a person's emotions and intentions, even if they are not speaking. For example, crossed arms or legs can indicate defensiveness, while an open posture can signal receptiveness.

It is worth noting that the relationship between the mind and body is not always a straightforward one. There are many factors that can impact the relationship between the two, including cultural background, individual personality, and life experiences. Nevertheless, the research in this area has made it clear that the mind and body are interconnected and that the way in which we use our bodies can have a significant impact on our thoughts and emotions.

The idea of a mind-body connection has been a topic of philosophical discussion for centuries. Descartes famously posited that the mind and body are distinct entities that interact, while others have argued that they are ultimately one and the same. Regardless of one's philosophical stance, it is clear that the relationship between the mind and body has a profound effect on human behavior.

One of the key ways in which the mind and body are connected is through the nervous system. The nervous system is responsible for transmitting signals from the brain to the rest of the body and vice versa. This means that our thoughts and emotions can have physical effects, such as changes in heart rate and blood pressure, as well as affecting our movements and bodily sensations.

Another way in which the mind and body are interconnected is through the endocrine system. The endocrine system releases hormones that have wide-ranging effects on the body, including regulating mood, energy levels, and metabolism. This means that our mental state can have a significant impact on our physical health, and vice versa. For example, stress can trigger the release of cortisol, a hormone that has been linked to weight gain and decreased immunity.

The connection between the mind and body can also affect our behavior in more subtle ways. For example, our thoughts and beliefs can impact our perception of pain. People who are more optimistic and have a more positive outlook on life tend to report less pain and experience less disability than those who are more pessimistic.

Moreover, the way we think about our bodies and physical health can impact our overall well-being. Research has shown that people who have a positive body image and view their bodies in a more accepting and appreciative light tend to have better physical health, improved mental health, and greater overall life satisfaction.

One approach to understanding the mind-body relationship is through the dualism perspective, which suggests that the mind and body are separate entities that interact with each other. This perspective posits that the mind has a non-physical essence and is capable of existing independently of the body, whereas the body is made up of physical matter. This theory has been debated for centuries, with some philosopher's suggesting that the mind and body are not separate entities but are rather two aspects of the same thing.

Another perspective is the materialist approach, which holds that the mind is a product of the physical activity of the brain and the nervous system. This approach suggests that mental states and experiences are emergent properties of the functioning of the brain and nervous system and cannot exist independently of them.

The relationship between the mind and body has significant implications for human behavior. For example, the dualism perspective suggests that behavior is the result of the interaction between the mind and the body, while the materialist approach posits that behavior is a direct result of the activity of the brain and nervous system. This difference in perspective leads to different explanations for a range of human behaviors, from psychological disorders to personal choices.

One area where the mind-body relationship has significant implications is in the field of psychology. The dualism perspective suggests that mental disorders, such as depression and anxiety, are the result of an imbalance in the interaction between the mind and the body. In contrast, the materialist approach suggests that mental disorders are a result of imbalances or malfunctions in the functioning of the brain and nervous system. This difference in perspective leads to different approaches to treating mental disorders, with some therapies focusing on improving the mind-body interaction, while others focus on addressing the underlying physical causes.

The mind-body relationship also has implications for personal choices and decision making. Dualism suggests that the mind has the ability to make decisions independent of the body, while the materialist approach suggests that decision making is the result of the physical activity of the brain. This difference in perspective may impact the way in which individuals understand and make decisions about their health, personal relationships, and life goals.

One of the most prominent theories in the relationship between the mind and the body is the dualism theory. This theory suggests that the mind and the body are separate entities, and that the mind is not just a function of the physical brain. The mind is seen as a non-physical entity that can exist independently of the body, and can affect the body in a number of ways. This theory has been widely debated, as it raises questions about the nature of consciousness, free will, and the morality of actions taken by the mind.

Another theory is the monism theory, which suggests that the mind and the body are not separate entities, but rather different aspects of the same entity. This theory suggests that the mind is simply the result of the activity of the brain, and that all mental processes are ultimately physical processes. There are two main forms of monism - materialism and idealism. Materialism suggests that all mental processes are the result of physical processes in the brain, while idealism suggests that all physical processes are the result of mental processes.

The relationship between the mind and the body has a significant impact on human behavior. For example, mental disorders such as depression and anxiety are thought to have a biological basis, and are often treated with both psychotherapy and medication. Additionally, the mind and the body are thought to have a mutual influence on each other. For example, stress can have a significant impact on physical health, and physical exercise can have a positive impact on mental health.

It is important to note that the relationship between the mind and the body is complex and not fully understood.

There are still many questions that remain unanswered, and much research is still being done in this field. Nevertheless, the study of the relationship between the mind and the body is an important area of study that has the potential to provide insight into a number of important questions about human behavior, including the nature of consciousness, the origins of mental disorders, and the effectiveness of various treatments.

In addition to the philosophical debate, there has been a growing body of scientific research on the relationship between the mind and the body. One of the key areas of investigation is the connection between physical and mental health. For example, studies have shown that chronic stress and anxiety can lead to physical symptoms such as headaches, fatigue, and muscle pain. Conversely, physical activity and exercise can improve mood and reduce symptoms of depression.

Another area of investigation is the effect of physical sensations on the brain. For example, studies have shown that the placebo effect is a real phenomenon, where the mere expectation of improvement can lead to actual physiological changes in the body. This suggests that the connection between the mind and the body is a two-way street, with each influencing the other.

The relationship between the mind and the body also has implications for human behavior. For example, research has shown that people with certain physical characteristics, such as height or body shape, are more likely to be successful in certain situations, such as leadership positions. Conversely, physical health problems, such as chronic pain, can impact mental health and behavior, leading to feelings of hopelessness and decreased motivation.

The relationship between the mind and the body is complex and multi-faceted. While there is still much to be learned, it is clear that understanding this relationship is crucial for improving health and wellbeing. Further research is needed to fully understand the intricacies of this connection and to develop effective interventions that can improve mental and physical health.

One way to examine the relationship between the mind and the body is through the study of cognitive neuroscience. Cognitive neuroscience seeks to understand how the brain and nervous system enable complex mental processes such as perception, attention, language, memory, and emotions. The relationship between the mind and the body is also studied in fields such as psychology, philosophy, and biology.

There are several theories that attempt to explain the relationship between the mind and the body, including dualism, materialism, and idealism. Dualism, popularized by philosopher René Descartes, argues that the mind and the body are separate entities that interact with each other. Materialism, on the other hand, suggests that the mind is a product of the physical brain and that mental processes can be reduced to physical processes. Idealism argues that the mind is not a product of the brain and that the physical world is dependent on the mental world.

Recent developments in brain imaging techniques such as magnetic resonance imaging (MRI) and positron emission tomography (PET) have enabled scientists to study the brain's structure and function in unprecedented detail. This has led to a better understanding of how the brain and the mind are related, and how mental processes are embodied in the physical brain.

However, there is still much that we do not understand about the relationship between the mind and the body, and how this relationship affects human behavior. For example, we do not yet fully understand how experiences, emotions, and thoughts are processed in the brain and how they influence behavior.

The relationship between the mind and the body also has significant ethical implications. For example, if the mind is a product of the brain, then it is possible to manipulate the mind through brain surgery or pharmacological means. This raises questions about personal autonomy, free will, and the limits of scientific and technological advancements. Additionally, if the mind and the body are separate entities, what happens to the mind after death? These are just a few of the many ethical questions that arise from the study of the relationship between the mind and the body.

Despite the challenges, it is clear that understanding the relationship between the mind and the body is of fundamental importance for advancing our knowledge of human behavior, the workings of the brain, and the nature of consciousness. As our understanding of this relationship continues to grow, it will likely lead to new and innovative treatments for mental and neurological disorders, as well as new technologies for enhancing human cognition and wellbeing.

It is widely accepted in the scientific community that the mind and body are intricately connected and that this connection has a significant impact on human behavior. The mind and body are not separate entities, but are interdependent and constantly influencing each other.

One of the most famous theories in the field of mind-body research is the psychosomatic model, which states that the mind and body are connected and that mental processes can directly impact physical health. For example, stress and anxiety have been linked to various health problems such as cardiovascular disease, gastrointestinal disorders, and immune system dysfunctions. In addition, research has shown that physical exercise and movement can have a positive impact on mental health, reducing symptoms of depression and anxiety.

Another area of research that sheds light on the relationship between the mind and body is the study of emotions. It is well established that emotions can have a profound impact on the body. For instance, when we experience fear, our heart rate and blood pressure increase, and when we experience happiness, our heart rate decreases and our blood pressure drops. Furthermore, emotions can also influence our behavior in significant ways. For example, anger and frustration can lead to aggressive behavior, while happiness and contentment can lead to prosocial behavior.

The relationship between the mind and body also affects human behavior through the regulation of neurotransmitters and hormones in the body. Neurotransmitters are chemicals in the brain that regulate mood, emotion, and cognition. Hormones, on the other hand, are chemicals that regulate various physiological processes such as metabolism, growth, and reproductive behavior. Research has shown that imbalances in neurotransmitters and hormones can lead to behavioral and emotional problems, such as depression and anxiety.

The mind-body relationship is a complex and interrelated dynamic that affects human behavior in a multitude of ways. It is often said that the mind is what controls the body, and this is certainly true to a large extent.

However, the body also plays a role in shaping the mind and our thoughts, feelings, and behavior. This relationship is known as the mind-body connection, and it is important to understand the ways in which the mind and body influence each other.

One example of this relationship can be seen in the study of the placebo effect, where a patient's belief that they have received medication can produce real physiological changes in their body. The mind-body connection is also evident in the field of psychosomatic medicine, where mental and emotional stress can manifest as physical symptoms such as headaches, back pain, and stomach problems. These examples show how the mind and body can affect each other, but the reverse is also true.

The physical state of the body can also affect our mental state, and this is particularly true in the case of exercise. Physical activity is known to release endorphins, which are natural chemicals that can boost our mood and improve our overall sense of well-being. Exercise has also been linked to the growth of new brain cells, which can help to improve our cognitive function and increase our mental agility.

The mind-body connection also has implications for mental health. A growing body of research suggests that mental disorders such as depression, anxiety, and PTSD may have a physiological component that can be targeted through treatments such as exercise, diet, and sleep. For example, studies have shown that physical activity can help to reduce symptoms of depression and anxiety, while sleep deprivation can increase the risk of depression and anxiety.

One approach to examining the relationship between the mind and the body is through the use of functional imaging techniques, such as functional magnetic resonance imaging (fMRI) and positron emission tomography (PET).

These techniques allow researchers to visualize the neural activity in the brain while individuals are engaged in various mental activities, such as problem-solving or decision-making. This has provided a wealth of information about the neural circuits involved in various cognitive processes and how they interact with the rest of the body.

Another approach to exploring the relationship between the mind and the body is through the study of mental disorders and the physiological changes that occur in the body as a result. For example, depression has been linked to changes in the levels of certain neurotransmitters in the brain and alterations in the activity of the hypothalamic-pituitary-adrenal (HPA) axis. Additionally, conditions such as anxiety and stress have been linked to changes in the functioning of the immune system, as well as changes in heart rate and blood pressure.

Finally, researchers are also exploring the relationship between the mind and the body through the study of behavioral and cognitive therapies. For example, mindfulness-based therapies, such as meditation and yoga, have been shown to have a positive impact on mental and physical health by reducing stress, improving sleep, and decreasing symptoms of depression and anxiety. Cognitive-behavioral therapy (CBT) has also been used to treat a wide range of mental health disorders and has been shown to be effective in reducing symptoms by changing the way people think about and respond to their experiences.

One philosophical approach that helps to understand the relationship between the mind and body is Dualism. Dualism posits that the mind and body are two separate entities that interact with each other, but are not reducible to one another. This idea has been popularized by René Descartes, who argued that the mind is a non-physical, thinking substance, while the body is a physical, material substance. Descartes believed that the mind could control the body through the pineal gland, which acted as a sort of bridge between the two.

Another philosophical approach is Materialism, which holds that the mind is nothing more than the workings of the brain and the body. Materialists argue that the mind can be reduced to the physical interactions between neurons and other bodily systems. This view was popularized by figures such as Thomas Hobbes and Julien Offray de La Mettrie.

In terms of how the mind-body relationship affects human behavior, many theorists have proposed that our thoughts, feelings, and beliefs can have a direct impact on our physical health. For example, studies have shown that chronic stress can increase the risk of heart disease, and that negative thought patterns can contribute to depression and anxiety. Similarly, it has been suggested that the placebo effect, where a person's belief in a treatment can have a positive impact on their health, is another example of the mind-body connection.

In recent years, the field of neuroplasticity has shed new light on the mind-body relationship. Researchers have discovered that the brain is capable of adapting and changing in response to new experiences and information, which can affect behavior. For example, a person who learns a new skill or habit can change the connections between neurons in their brain, which can lead to changes in behavior.

Finally, the mind-body relationship is also related to the concept of consciousness. Consciousness refers to the subjective experience of being aware of one's thoughts, feelings, and surroundings. While there is still much debate about the nature of consciousness, some theories suggest that it emerges from the physical interactions between the brain and the body. Others argue that consciousness is a non-physical, spiritual entity that transcends the physical world.

The mind-body relationship is also explored through the concept of mindfulness and meditation. Practicing mindfulness and meditation has been shown to have physical benefits, such as reducing inflammation and improving heart health, as well as mental benefits, such as reducing stress and improving emotional regulation. This relationship between the mind and body is further evidenced by the placebo effect, where a patient's belief in a treatment can have a real impact on their physical symptoms. Additionally, studies have shown that chronic stress can lead to physical health problems, such as heart disease, and that stress management techniques can have a positive impact on physical health.

It is also important to consider the implications of the mind-body relationship for mental health disorders. Mental health disorders, such as depression and anxiety, can have physical symptoms, such as changes in appetite or sleep patterns, and can also impact physical health, such as through increased risk of heart disease. Treatment for mental health disorders often involves a combination of medication and therapy, with the goal of addressing both the physical and mental aspects of the disorder.

The study of the mind-body relationship has implications for many fields, including psychology, neuroscience, and medicine. Further research in this area can help us to better understand the complex interplay between the mind and body and how this relationship affects human behavior. In turn, this understanding can inform the development of new and more effective treatments for mental and physical health problems.

The relationship between the mind and body is a complex and multi-faceted subject that has been the subject of philosophical and scientific inquiry for centuries. The mind-body problem, as it is known, is the question of how mental states and processes are related to physical states and processes in the body. There are two main philosophical perspectives on this relationship: dualism and monism.

Dualism is the idea that the mind and body are separate and distinct entities, and that the mind can exist without the body. This view was popularized by the philosopher René Descartes, who argued that the mind and body interact with each other through the pineal gland in the brain. According to this view, the mind and body have different properties and are not subject to the same laws of physics.

Monism, on the other hand, is the view that there is only one substance, either physical or mental, that constitutes the universe. This view holds that the mind and body are not separate entities, but rather that the mind is a product of the brain and nervous system. Proponents of this view argue that the mind is simply a particular type of physical process that emerges from the functioning of the brain and nervous system.

Recent advances in neuroscience and psychology have provided further insights into the relationship between the mind and body. For example, research in the field of cognitive neuroscience has shown that mental processes such as perception, attention, and memory are closely tied to specific regions of the brain. This has led to the development of brain-computer interfaces, which allow people to control computers and other devices with their thoughts.

The relationship between the mind and body also has important implications for our understanding of human behavior. For example, the mind-body connection can help us understand why certain physical or environmental factors, such as stress, can have a significant impact on our mental health and well-being. On the other hand, mental states and processes, such as emotions, can also have a significant impact on physical health.

The mind-body relationship has been a subject of much debate and discussion among philosophers, scientists, and scholars for centuries. The connection between the mind and the body has been described in various ways, ranging from a simple correlation to an interdependent relationship. While the concept of mind-body dualism suggests that the mind and body are separate entities, many researchers have rejected this notion and instead propose that the mind and body are intimately connected.

One important aspect of the mind-body relationship is the impact of the physical body on the mind. Studies have shown that physical exercise can have a significant impact on mental health and well-being, reducing symptoms of anxiety and depression. This has led many to believe that the body and mind are intricately connected, and that changes in the physical state of the body can affect the mental state of an individual.

Another aspect of the mind-body relationship is the impact of the mind on the body. For instance, stress can cause physical symptoms, such as headaches, muscle tension, and digestive issues. Additionally, emotions, such as anger, fear, and joy, can also impact physical health. Research has shown that negative emotions can trigger the release of stress hormones, which can be harmful to the body over time.

The impact of the mind-body relationship on human behavior is significant. For example, when the body experiences stress, the mind may respond by seeking relief through addictive behaviors such as substance abuse or overeating. Similarly, physical pain or discomfort may result in irritability and mood swings, affecting an individual's behavior.

In conclusion, the relationship between the mind and the body is a complex and multi-faceted topic that has been the subject of much debate and research for centuries. While the exact nature of this relationship is still not fully understood, it is clear that the two are intricately connected and influence each other in numerous ways. How this relationship affects human behavior is also a complex issue, with many factors involved, including both genetic and environmental factors. Ultimately, the relationship between the mind and the body is an important area of study that holds much potential for advancing our understanding of human behavior and psychology. Further research into this topic will help us better understand the mechanisms underlying this relationship and may lead to the development of more effective treatments for mental health issues and other behavioral disorders.

CHAPTER FOUR

What is dark matter, and what role does it play in the universe?

The universe is a vast and complex system that has fascinated scientists and researchers for centuries. One of the most intriguing mysteries of the universe is the presence of dark matter, which accounts for a significant portion of the universe's mass but does not emit or absorb light or other forms of electromagnetic radiation. In this research paper, we will explore the concept of dark matter, its properties, and the role it plays in the universe.

Background:

The concept of dark matter was first proposed in the 1930s by Swiss astronomer Fritz Zwicky, who observed that the mass of visible matter in the Coma Cluster of galaxies was not sufficient to account for the cluster's gravitational force. He proposed that the missing mass was in the form of invisible matter, which he termed "dark matter." Subsequent studies of the rotation curves of galaxies and the cosmic microwave background radiation have provided further evidence for the existence of dark matter.

Properties of Dark Matter:

Dark matter is defined as matter that does not interact with electromagnetic radiation and cannot be detected through telescopes or other traditional astronomical instruments. However, its presence can be inferred through its gravitational effects on visible matter. Dark matter is believed to make up about 85% of the matter in the universe, with visible matter accounting for the remaining 15%.

The exact nature of dark matter is still unknown, but several theories have been proposed. One of the most widely accepted theories is that dark matter is made up of weakly interacting massive particles (WIMPs). WIMPs are particles that do not interact with electromagnetic radiation but do interact through the weak nuclear force, which is responsible for radioactive decay.

Role of Dark Matter in the Universe:

The presence of dark matter plays a crucial role in the structure and evolution of the universe. Without dark matter, galaxies and other large structures would not be able to form and maintain their shape. Dark matter provides the gravitational force necessary to hold galaxies together, as well as the "scaffolding" on which galaxies and other structures can form.

In addition, dark matter plays a crucial role in the evolution of the universe as a whole. The distribution of dark matter in the early universe influenced the formation of visible matter, leading to the large-scale structures we observe today. Dark matter also affects the expansion rate of the universe and the distribution of galaxies.

Current Research and Observations:

Scientists are constantly searching for new ways to study dark matter, and recent research has provided some new insights into this mysterious substance. For example, a study published in the journal Science in 2020 used observations of gravitational lensing to create a high-resolution map of the distribution of dark matter in a massive galaxy cluster. The study found that the dark matter in the cluster was distributed more smoothly than previously thought, which could help to refine our understanding of the properties of dark matter.

Another recent study, published in the journal Nature in 2021, used data from the Dark Energy Survey to create a map of the distribution of dark matter in the universe. The study found that the distribution of dark matter was consistent with the predictions of the standard cosmological model, which suggests that dark matter is made up of WIMPs.

In addition to observational studies, researchers are also exploring new theoretical models of dark matter. For example, some researchers have proposed that dark matter could be made up of sterile neutrinos, which are hypothetical particles that interact only through gravity and the weak nuclear force. Other models propose that dark matter is made up of axions, which are particles that have very little mass and interact very weakly with other matter.

The Future of Dark Matter Research:

Despite decades of research, many questions about dark matter remain unanswered. In the coming years, researchers will continue to explore new observations and theoretical models in an effort to better understand this mysterious substance. One promising approach is to search for dark matter particles directly, using highly sensitive detectors that are designed to detect the weak signals produced by interactions between dark matter and normal matter.

Another approach is to study the cosmic microwave background radiation, which provides a snapshot of the universe at a very early stage in its history. By studying the patterns in the radiation, researchers can learn more about the distribution of dark matter in the early universe and how it influenced the formation of visible matter.

Challenges in Studying Dark Matter:

One of the biggest challenges in studying dark matter is its elusive nature. Because it does not interact with electromagnetic radiation, it is very difficult to detect or observe directly. Instead, researchers must rely on indirect methods, such as studying its gravitational effects on visible matter or searching for dark matter particles.

Another challenge is that dark matter is thought to interact only weakly with other matter, which makes it very difficult to detect. Even if dark matter particles are produced in experiments, they may be very difficult to detect because their interactions with other matter are so weak.

A third challenge is that the exact nature of dark matter is still unknown. While the WIMP model is widely accepted, it is still a theoretical construct, and other models of dark matter are still being explored. Without a clear understanding of the nature of dark matter, it is difficult to design experiments or observations that can detect or study it.

Implications of Dark Matter:

The study of dark matter has important implications for our understanding of the universe as a whole. For example, the distribution of dark matter can provide insights into the early universe and how large-scale structures like galaxies formed. Understanding dark matter can also help us to better understand the fundamental forces that govern the behavior of matter and energy in the universe.

In addition, understanding the properties of dark matter is important for our understanding of the future of the universe. Because dark matter provides the gravitational force that holds galaxies together, its distribution will ultimately determine the fate of the universe. If the universe contains enough dark matter, its gravitational pull will eventually halt the expansion of the universe and cause it to collapse in a "big crunch." If there is not enough dark matter, the universe will continue to expand indefinitely.

Alternative Theories and Debates:

Despite the widespread acceptance of the WIMP model, some researchers have proposed alternative theories of dark matter. For example, some researchers have suggested that dark matter is not made up of particles at all, but is instead a modification of the laws of gravity at large scales. This theory, known as Modified Newtonian Dynamics (MOND), suggests that the gravitational force between objects is stronger than predicted by the standard laws of gravity.

However, the MOND theory has not been widely accepted, as it does not explain some of the observed effects of dark matter, such as gravitational lensing. Other theories propose that dark matter is made up of particles that are much lighter than WIMPs, such as axions or sterile neutrinos.

In addition, some researchers have questioned whether dark matter exists at all. While the evidence for dark matter is compelling, some have suggested that the observed effects could be explained by other phenomena, such as small black holes or modifications to the laws of gravity.

The Role of Dark Matter in Galaxy Formation:

One of the most important roles of dark matter is in the formation of galaxies. According to the prevailing model of galaxy formation, dark matter acts as a scaffolding on which visible matter can accumulate. As dark matter particles gravitate towards each other, they form halos of dark matter that provide the gravitational force needed to pull in gas and dust. As this gas and dust accumulates, it eventually collapses to form stars and galaxies.

While the precise details of galaxy formation are still being explored, the role of dark matter in this process is widely accepted. Without the gravitational force provided by dark matter, it is unlikely that galaxies could have formed and evolved as they have.

Dark Matter Detection Experiments:

Despite the challenges of detecting dark matter, several experiments are currently underway to try and detect dark matter particles directly. One of the most well-known experiments is the Large Underground Xenon (LUX) experiment, which is located in a mine in South Dakota. The LUX experiment uses a tank filled with liquid xenon, which is designed to detect the faint signals that would be produced by a dark matter particle interacting with the xenon atoms.

Another experiment is the Dark Energy Survey (DES), which is designed to study both dark energy and dark matter. The DES uses a large camera mounted on a telescope in Chile to map the distribution of dark matter across a large region of the sky.

Other experiments include the Super Cryogenic Dark Matter Search (SuperCDMS), the Axion Dark Matter Experiment (ADMX), and the Cosmic Axion Spin

Precession Experiment (CASPEr). Each of these experiments is designed to detect different types of dark matter particles and uses different detection methods.

The Future of Dark Matter Research:

As researchers continue to study dark matter, new observations and experimental results are likely to shed light on its properties and behavior. For example, the upcoming Vera C. Rubin Observatory, which is expected to begin operations in 2023, will be able to map the distribution of dark matter across a large portion of the sky.

In addition, researchers are exploring new experimental techniques that may be able to detect dark matter particles directly. These include using high-energy particle accelerators to produce dark matter particles, as well as new types of detectors that can sense very faint signals.

Finally, the search for dark matter is closely connected to other areas of research, such as particle physics and cosmology. As our understanding of these fields improves, we can expect to gain a better understanding of dark matter and its role in the universe.

The Search for Dark Matter Candidates:

In the search for dark matter candidates, researchers have proposed several possible particles that could make up dark matter. One of the most promising candidates is the WIMP, or Weakly Interacting Massive Particle, which is a hypothetical particle that interacts very weakly with normal matter. WIMPs are predicted by some models of particle physics, but have not yet been detected directly.

Other potential dark matter candidates include axions, sterile neutrinos, and gravitinos. Axions are hypothetical particles that were originally proposed to explain why the strong nuclear force does not violate the symmetry of time. However, they are also a possible dark matter candidate, as they would interact very weakly with normal matter.

Sterile neutrinos are similar to regular neutrinos, but do not interact with other particles through the weak nuclear force. Gravitinos are hypothetical particles that are predicted by some theories of supersymmetry, a proposed extension of the standard model of particle physics.

While these particles are all potential dark matter candidates, none of them have been detected directly, and the search for dark matter particles continues.

Theoretical Models of Dark Matter:

In addition to the search for dark matter particles, researchers are also developing theoretical models to explain the behavior and properties of dark matter. One popular model is the Lambda Cold Dark Matter (ΛCDM) model, which predicts that dark matter is distributed in halos around galaxies and that it interacts only weakly with normal matter.

However, some observations of galaxies and galaxy clusters suggest that the distribution of dark matter is more complex than predicted by the ΛCDM model. This has led to the development of alternative models, such as the Self-Interacting Dark Matter (SIDM) model, which proposes that dark matter particles interact with each other through a new type of force.

Other models propose that dark matter is made up of particles that interact with normal matter through a new type of force, which would allow dark matter to interact more strongly with normal matter than previously thought.

The Role of Dark Matter in Cosmology:

Finally, dark matter plays an important role in our understanding of the universe on the largest scales. According to the prevailing model of cosmology, the universe began with the Big Bang, and has been expanding ever since. Dark matter is thought to have played a key role in the formation of the large-scale structure of the universe, such as galaxies and galaxy clusters.

In addition, the observed distribution of dark matter provides important information about the overall structure and evolution of the universe. By studying the distribution of dark matter and its interactions with normal matter, researchers can gain insights into the fundamental forces that govern the behavior of matter and energy.

Dark Matter Detection:

While dark matter has not been directly observed, there are several ways in which its presence can be inferred. One method is to observe the effects of gravitational lensing, where the gravity of a massive object, such as a galaxy, bends and distorts the light of more distant objects. By studying the amount and distribution of gravitational lensing in a given area, researchers can infer the presence of dark matter.

Another method is to study the motion of stars and gas in galaxies and galaxy clusters. The observed motion of these objects cannot be explained by the gravitational pull of visible matter alone, indicating the presence of additional mass in the form of dark matter.

Several experiments have also been designed to directly detect dark matter particles. One such experiment is the Large Hadron Collider (LHC) at CERN, which collides particles at high energies in an attempt to create and detect new particles, including potential dark matter candidates. Another experiment is the Cryogenic Dark Matter Search (CDMS), which uses ultra-cold detectors to search for the weak signals of dark matter particle interactions with normal matter.

The hunt for dark matter continues to be a major focus of research in astrophysics and particle physics, with new experiments and technologies being developed to probe the properties and nature of dark matter.

Implications for Cosmology:

The presence of dark matter has important implications for our understanding of the evolution and structure of the universe. One of the most significant implications is the role of dark matter in the formation of galaxies and galaxy clusters.

According to the prevailing model of cosmology, small fluctuations in the density of matter in the early universe grew over time through the force of gravity, eventually forming the large-scale structures we observe today. However, this model only works if the matter in the universe is not evenly distributed, but instead is clumped into halos of dark matter.

The distribution and behavior of dark matter also provides important information about the fundamental nature of the universe. For example, some theories of particle physics predict the existence of additional dimensions beyond the three we experience, which could have important implications for the behavior of dark matter.

Finally, the search for dark matter has the potential to fundamentally alter our understanding of the universe and the nature of matter and energy. By uncovering the properties and behavior of dark matter, researchers may be able to develop new technologies and insights into the fundamental laws of the universe.

Dark Matter and Dark Energy:

While dark matter is an important component of the universe, it is not the only one. Another mysterious substance, known as dark energy, is believed to be responsible for the accelerating expansion of the universe.

Unlike dark matter, which exerts a gravitational pull that slows the expansion of the universe, dark energy is a hypothetical form of energy that permeates all of space and exerts a repulsive force that drives the expansion of the universe.

The nature and properties of dark energy are still largely unknown, and its existence is inferred from observations of the large-scale structure of the universe and the cosmic microwave background radiation. The leading hypothesis for dark energy is that it is a form of vacuum energy associated with the fabric of space-time itself.

The relationship between dark matter and dark energy is still a subject of active research, and their coexistence has important implications for the evolution and fate of the universe.

The Future of Dark Matter Research:

The study of dark matter is a rapidly evolving field, with new discoveries and advancements being made all the time. One of the most exciting areas of research is the search for new dark matter particles and the development of more sensitive detectors.

Another area of research is the study of dark matter in the early universe, which could provide clues about the fundamental nature of dark matter and its role in the formation of structure in the universe.

The use of computer simulations and advanced data analysis techniques is also becoming increasingly important in the study of dark matter. By modeling the behavior and distribution of dark matter, researchers can test different theoretical models and make predictions about the observable properties of dark matter.

The study of dark matter also has important implications for the search for life beyond Earth. The distribution of dark matter in the Milky Way and other galaxies could play a role in the habitability of other planets, and the properties of dark matter could impact the search for extraterrestrial life.

Dark Matter and the Search for New Physics:

The study of dark matter is closely linked to the search for new physics beyond the Standard Model of particle physics. The Standard Model is a well-tested theory that describes the behavior of subatomic particles and their interactions, but it does not include a viable candidate for dark matter.

As a result, many physicists believe that the discovery of dark matter will require the development of new theories and models that go beyond the Standard Model. These theories could include new particles, new forces, and even new dimensions of space-time.

Some proposed models of dark matter include Weakly Interacting Massive Particles (WIMPs), Axions, and sterile neutrinos. The search for these particles and others like them is a major focus of experimental and theoretical research.

In addition to providing a solution to the dark matter problem, the discovery of new particles and forces could have important implications for other areas of physics, including the unification of the fundamental forces and the nature of dark energy.

Dark Matter and the Large-Scale Structure of the Universe:

The distribution of dark matter in the universe plays a key role in the formation and evolution of large-scale structures such as galaxies and galaxy clusters. In particular, the clumping of dark matter into halos is thought to be the seed for the formation of galaxies and other structures.

Observations of the large-scale structure of the universe, such as the distribution of galaxies and the cosmic microwave background radiation, provide important constraints on the properties and behavior of dark matter.

The distribution of dark matter also provides important clues about the early universe and the conditions that existed in the moments after the Big Bang. By studying the cosmic microwave background radiation and the large-scale distribution of matter, researchers can gain insights into the fundamental nature of the universe and the physics that governed its early evolution.

The study of dark matter is a complex and multifaceted field that has important implications for our understanding of the universe. From the search for new particles to the study of large-scale structures, researchers are making progress in unraveling the mysteries of dark matter and its role in the cosmos. The continued investigation of dark matter promises to yield new discoveries and insights into the fundamental nature of the universe.

The Role of Dark Matter in Galactic Dynamics:

One of the most compelling pieces of evidence for the existence of dark matter is its role in the dynamics of galaxies. The visible matter in galaxies, such as stars and gas, is not sufficient to explain the observed rotation curves of galaxies.

Rotation curves describe how the orbital speed of stars and gas changes with distance from the center of a galaxy. In a typical spiral galaxy, the rotation curve should decrease as distance from the center increases, just as the velocity of a planet decreases as it moves away from the sun. However, observations show that the rotation curves of galaxies remain flat, indicating that there must be more mass present than is visible.

The most likely explanation for the observed rotation curves is the presence of a large amount of invisible matter, or dark matter, that exerts a gravitational pull on the visible matter. The distribution of dark matter in galaxies is thought to be dominated by a halo, a spherical region that surrounds the visible matter and extends far beyond it.

The study of galactic dynamics is an important area of research in dark matter, as it provides important constraints on the properties and behavior of dark matter. The distribution of dark matter in galaxies can be studied through a variety of observational techniques, including the measurement of gravitational lensing, the study of galactic rotation curves, and the analysis of the large-scale distribution of matter.

Dark Matter and the Search for Dark Stars:

Another intriguing possibility for the role of dark matter is the formation of dark stars. Dark stars are theoretical objects that are powered by the annihilation of dark matter particles, rather than by nuclear fusion.

Dark stars could form in the early universe, when the density of dark matter was much higher than it is today. The high density of dark matter would cause the particles to annihilate and produce large amounts of heat, which could ignite a dark star.

The study of dark stars is still largely theoretical, and the existence of these objects has not yet been confirmed. However, the possibility of their existence is an exciting area of research in dark matter, as it could provide important insights into the nature and behavior of dark matter.

Dark Matter and the Formation of Large-Scale Structures:

In addition to its role in galactic dynamics, dark matter also plays a crucial role in the formation of large-scale structures in the universe. Observations of the cosmic microwave background radiation and the large-scale distribution of galaxies reveal a pattern of fluctuations in the density of matter that is consistent with the existence of dark matter.

These density fluctuations would have been present in the early universe, and as the universe expanded and cooled, the denser regions would have begun to collapse under their own gravity, eventually forming clusters and superclusters of galaxies.

The process of structure formation is influenced by the properties of dark matter, including its distribution and interactions with other matter. The study of large-scale structure formation provides important constraints on the properties of dark matter, as well as insights into the evolution of the universe as a whole.

Dark Matter and the Nature of the Universe:

The study of dark matter also has important implications for our understanding of the nature of the universe. The existence of dark matter suggests that there is more to the universe than what is visible, and that the visible matter is only a small fraction of the total matter content.

Furthermore, the properties of dark matter provide important constraints on theories of particle physics and the behavior of matter at the smallest scales. Dark matter is thought to be a type of particle that interacts only weakly with other matter, and the search for new dark matter particles is an important area of research in particle physics.

The study of dark matter also has important implications for our understanding of the ultimate fate of the universe. The distribution of dark matter affects the rate of expansion of the universe, and could determine whether the universe will continue to expand indefinitely or eventually collapse in a Big Crunch.

Overall, the study of dark matter is an important and exciting area of research that has far-reaching implications for our understanding of the universe. While many questions about dark matter remain unanswered, continued research and observation are sure to yield new insights and discoveries in the years to come.

Dark Matter and the Early Universe:

One of the key pieces of evidence for the existence of dark matter comes from observations of the cosmic microwave background (CMB), which is radiation left over from the early universe. The CMB provides a snapshot of the universe when it was just 380,000 years old, and it contains information about the distribution of matter at that time.

Analysis of the CMB has shown that the distribution of matter in the early universe was not smooth, but instead had small fluctuations. These fluctuations were caused by the gravitational pull of slightly denser regions of matter, and they are thought to be the seeds that grew into the large-scale structure of the universe we see today.

The pattern of these fluctuations in the CMB can be used to infer the total amount of matter in the universe, and it is estimated that dark matter makes up around 27% of the total matter in the universe. The remaining 5% is made up of visible matter, while the remaining 68% is dark energy.

Understanding the role of dark matter in the early universe is a key goal of modern cosmology, and ongoing research is shedding new light on this mysterious component of the universe.

Dark Matter and Galaxy Formation:

One of the most important roles of dark matter is in the formation of galaxies. According to the current model of galaxy formation, dark matter played a critical role in the early stages of the universe, providing the gravitational attraction that allowed gas and dust to accumulate and form the first protogalaxies.

Over time, these protogalaxies merged and evolved into the galaxies we see today. The distribution of dark matter in the universe also plays a key role in shaping the large-scale structure of the universe, influencing the distribution of galaxies and galaxy clusters.

The relationship between dark matter and visible matter in galaxies is also of great interest to astronomers. While dark matter dominates the gravitational attraction in galaxies, visible matter plays a key role in the dynamics and evolution of galaxies.

Ongoing research is shedding new light on the relationship between dark matter and visible matter in galaxies, and is improving our understanding of the complex processes that shape the evolution of these fascinating objects.

In conclusion, dark matter is a mysterious component of the universe that makes up the majority of matter and plays a critical role in shaping the large-scale structure of the universe. Despite decades of research and observation, we still have much to learn about the properties and behavior of dark matter. However, ongoing research and observation, particularly in areas such as galaxy formation and the early universe, are providing new insights and clues that may help us unravel this cosmic mystery. Ultimately, a better understanding of dark matter is key to understanding the evolution of the universe and the fundamental nature of matter itself, and the study of dark matter remains one of the most exciting and promising areas of research in modern science.

CHAPTER FIVE

How do plants and animals adapt to their environments, and what role does evolution play?

Plants and animals have evolved over millions of years to adapt to their environments. The process of adaptation is driven by the principles of evolution, where populations change over time in response to environmental pressures, resulting in changes in physical and behavioral traits. The ability of organisms to adapt to their environment is crucial for their survival and success in the wild. In this paper, we will explore the mechanisms of adaptation in plants and animals and the role of evolution in this process.

Mechanisms of Adaptation in Plants:

Plants have a wide range of adaptations to survive in various environments. One of the most common adaptations is the ability to tolerate extreme temperatures.

For example, desert plants have adapted to survive in arid environments by developing deep roots to reach underground water sources, waxy coatings on their leaves to reduce water loss, and spines to deter herbivores. Additionally, some plants have evolved to rely on wind or animal pollination rather than relying on insects or birds for pollination.

Plants also adapt to changes in their surroundings by altering their growth and development. For example, some plants grow towards sources of light to maximize their photosynthesis, while others grow towards the shade to avoid overheating. Plants can also change their physiology to adapt to nutrient-poor soils by developing specialized root systems that can extract nutrients more efficiently.

Mechanisms of Adaptation in Animals:

Animals also have a range of adaptations to survive in their environments. One of the most common adaptations is camouflage. Camouflage allows animals to blend into their surroundings, making it more difficult for predators to spot them. Some animals also have the ability to change their coloration to match their surroundings, a process known as color change.

Another important adaptation in animals is the ability to store energy. Animals in colder climates, for example, store fat to help them survive long periods of time without food. Similarly, animals in arid environments have adapted to survive long periods of drought by storing water in specialized tissues.

The Role of Evolution in Adaptation:

The process of adaptation in plants and animals is driven by the principles of evolution. Over time, individuals with traits that are better suited to their environment are more likely to survive and reproduce, passing on these advantageous traits to their offspring. This process, known as natural selection, leads to changes in populations over time.

Evolution can occur through a variety of mechanisms, including mutation, genetic drift, and gene flow. Mutation introduces new genetic variations into a population, which can then be selected for or against depending on their usefulness. Genetic drift occurs when random events, such as natural disasters, lead to changes in the frequency of particular traits in a population. Gene flow occurs when individuals from different populations interbreed, leading to the exchange of genetic material and potential adaptation.

In addition to the adaptation of plants and animals to their environments, evolution also plays a significant role in shaping the diversity of life on Earth. Evolution is the process of change over time that occurs in populations of organisms. It is driven by the forces of natural selection, genetic drift, mutation, and gene flow.

Natural selection is the primary mechanism of evolution. It is a process that results in certain traits becoming more common in a population over time. The basic idea of natural selection is that individuals with certain traits are better adapted to their environment and are more likely to survive and reproduce than individuals without those traits. As a result, the traits that confer an advantage are passed on to the next generation, increasing their frequency in the population.

Genetic drift and mutation are also important forces in evolution. Genetic drift is the random fluctuations in allele frequencies in a population over time. This can occur in small populations or during a bottleneck event, where a large population is reduced to a small number of individuals. Mutation is the process by which genetic information is altered or added to a genome. Mutations can be harmful, neutral, or beneficial, and they provide the raw material for evolution.

Finally, gene flow is the movement of genetic material between populations. This can occur through migration or the movement of seeds or pollen. Gene flow can increase genetic diversity within a population and reduce differences between populations.

One example of how plants and animals adapt to their environments is through the process of coevolution. Coevolution is the reciprocal adaptation of two or more species to each other over time. A classic example of coevolution is the relationship between flowering plants and their pollinators, such as bees and butterflies. Over time, plants have evolved flowers with specific shapes, colors, and fragrances to attract specific pollinators, while pollinators have evolved specialized body parts to efficiently gather nectar and pollen from the flowers.

Another example of adaptation is seen in the physical structures of animals, such as the beaks of birds. Darwin observed that different species of finches on the Galapagos Islands had differently shaped beaks depending on the type of food they ate. This was a clear example of natural selection in action, where the beaks that were best suited to each type of food were passed on to future generations.

Adaptation can also occur at the molecular level. For example, bacteria have been observed to develop resistance to antibiotics through a process of natural selection. As bacteria reproduce, they may acquire mutations that enable them to survive in the presence of antibiotics. Over time, the resistant bacteria become more common in the population.

Evolution is not just a historical process, but an ongoing one. The study of evolution and adaptation in plants and animals can help us understand the relationships between species and how they are influenced by environmental factors. It can also inform conservation efforts and help us anticipate and respond to the effects of environmental change on species and ecosystems.

In addition to physical structures and molecular adaptations, plants and animals can also adapt to their environments through behavioral changes. For example, animals may change their feeding or hunting patterns in response to changes in the availability of food or the presence of predators. Some plants can adjust their growth patterns or photosynthesis rates to optimize their use of available resources, such as light and water.

Adaptation can also occur through population-level changes over time. Genetic variation within a population provides the raw material for natural selection to act upon. Individuals with certain traits that are better suited to their environment are more likely to survive and reproduce, passing those beneficial traits on to their offspring. Over generations, the frequency of those traits may increase within the population, leading to a population-level adaptation to the environment.

However, adaptation is not always a smooth or guaranteed process. Environmental changes can occur rapidly, and some species may not be able to adapt quickly enough to survive. This can lead to population declines or even extinction. Climate change, habitat loss, and other human activities are putting increasing pressure on many plant and animal species, highlighting the importance of understanding and studying adaptation in the natural world.

The study of adaptation and evolution has also broader implications for our understanding of life on Earth and beyond. The processes of adaptation and natural selection are not unique to our planet, and may be important factors in the evolution of life elsewhere in the universe. Studying adaptation and evolution can therefore help us better understand the potential for life beyond our planet, as well as our place in the natural world here on Earth.

One important aspect of adaptation and evolution is the concept of coevolution, which refers to the reciprocal adaptation of two or more species to each other. For example, some plants have evolved specialized structures to attract certain pollinators, while those pollinators have evolved specialized behaviors to obtain nectar from those plants. Similarly, some prey species have evolved defenses against their predators, while those predators have evolved strategies to overcome those defenses.

Coevolution can also occur between different populations or species in the same environment. For example, different populations of the same species may evolve different adaptations to better exploit different habitats or resources, leading to the development of new subspecies or even new species over time. Similarly, interactions between different species in the same environment can drive the evolution of new adaptations and ecological niches.

The study of adaptation and evolution also has important practical applications. By understanding the genetic and molecular mechanisms underlying adaptation, scientists can develop new strategies for crop improvement, disease resistance, and environmental conservation. The identification of key genetic markers or traits associated with adaptation can also help identify populations or species that are at risk of decline or extinction, and inform conservation efforts to protect them.

One fascinating area of research in the study of adaptation and evolution is the role of epigenetics, which refers to changes in gene expression that occur without changes to the underlying DNA sequence. Epigenetic modifications can be influenced by environmental factors, such as diet, stress, and exposure to toxins, and can be passed down to offspring.

Research has shown that epigenetic changes can play an important role in adaptation and evolution. For example, studies have found that exposure to environmental stressors can lead to changes in gene expression in plants, which can confer new traits that enable them to better survive and reproduce in those conditions. Similarly, researchers have found that epigenetic changes can be passed down to offspring, potentially allowing them to inherit adaptations from their parents.

Another area of research in the study of adaptation and evolution is the role of gene flow, or the movement of genes between different populations. Gene flow can have important consequences for the genetic diversity and adaptation of populations. For example, gene flow can increase genetic diversity within a population, which can enhance the ability of the population to adapt to changing environmental conditions. On the other hand, gene flow can also reduce genetic differences between populations, which can limit the ability of populations to adapt to local environmental conditions and potentially lead to the loss of locally adapted traits.

Finally, the study of adaptation and evolution also has important implications for understanding and predicting the impacts of global change on the natural world. As climate change, habitat loss, and other human activities continue to alter the planet, it is becoming increasingly important to understand how different species will adapt to these changing conditions. By studying the processes of adaptation and evolution, we can develop more effective strategies for conserving biodiversity and protecting the natural systems that support life on Earth.

In addition to physical adaptations, organisms also undergo behavioral adaptations to better suit their environments. For example, some animals, such as birds, migrate to warmer climates during the winter to avoid the harsh conditions of their original habitats. Similarly, some plants have evolved to only bloom during certain times of the year to ensure their pollinators are present.

Evolution also plays a significant role in the adaptation of organisms. Over time, genetic mutations and natural selection can lead to new traits that better suit an organism's environment. This can ultimately lead to the emergence of new species.

It is important to note that while adaptation and evolution allow organisms to better survive in their environments, they do not necessarily guarantee survival. Environmental changes, such as climate change and habitat destruction, can have significant impacts on the survival of many species. As such, conservation efforts are important to ensure the continued survival of these species and the preservation of biodiversity.

One example of how plants have adapted to their environments is the development of root systems. In arid regions, many plants have evolved deep root systems that allow them to reach groundwater sources, while in areas with heavy rainfall, plants may have evolved shallow roots to more easily access nutrients in the topsoil. Additionally, some plants have evolved specialized root structures, such as prop roots, that provide additional support in areas with strong winds or heavy rain.

Another example of adaptation in animals is the development of camouflage. Many animals have evolved coloration and patterns that help them blend into their surroundings, making them less visible to predators or prey. Similarly, some animals have evolved the ability to mimic other species in order to avoid detection.

The process of evolution is also important for the development of antibiotic resistance in bacteria. Over time, bacteria can develop mutations that allow them to resist the effects of antibiotics. This is a significant problem in modern medicine, as many bacterial infections are becoming increasingly difficult to treat.

In addition to the scientific implications of adaptation and evolution, these processes also have cultural and societal impacts. For example, many Indigenous cultures around the world have developed traditional knowledge and practices that incorporate an understanding of the natural world and the processes of adaptation and evolution.

To further discuss the topic of how plants and animals adapt to their environments and the role of evolution, it is important to consider some specific examples of adaptations that have evolved over time.

One well-known example of animal adaptation is the development of wings in birds. It is believed that the evolution of feathers in birds initially served as insulation, but eventually led to the development of wings that allowed birds to fly. Over time, birds with longer wings and more aerodynamic shapes were more successful in flight and were better adapted to their environment. This is an example of natural selection at work, where the fittest individuals are more likely to survive and reproduce.

Another example of animal adaptation is seen in the polar bear, which has evolved to survive in the harsh Arctic environment. The polar bear's thick fur and layer of blubber provide insulation against the cold, while its large paws allow it to walk on ice and swim in the water. The bear's white fur also serves as camouflage, allowing it to blend in with its snowy surroundings and hunt effectively.

In terms of plant adaptations, a notable example is the evolution of succulent plants, such as cacti. These plants have thick, fleshy leaves and stems that store water, allowing them to survive in arid environments. The presence of spines on the surface of the plant also helps to deter herbivores from eating the plant and damaging its ability to survive.

Overall, these examples demonstrate how adaptations in plants and animals have allowed them to successfully adapt to their environments over time. Evolution plays a crucial role in this process, as genetic variations that confer a survival advantage are passed down from one generation to the next. As the environment changes, those individuals that are better adapted to the new conditions are more likely to survive and pass on their genes to future generations.

It is important to note that while adaptations can be beneficial for an individual organism, they do not always lead to long-term success. For example, an adaptation that is effective in one environment may not be useful in another environment, which can limit the range of habitats in which a species can survive. Additionally, some adaptations may be beneficial in the short term but have negative consequences in the long term, such as the development of antibiotic resistance in bacteria.

One way in which animals and plants can adapt to their environment is through phenotypic plasticity. This is the ability of an organism to modify its physical or physiological traits in response to changes in the environment. For example, some plants may produce more root mass to access more water if they experience drought, or animals may produce more melanin to protect against UV radiation.

Another way in which organisms adapt to their environment is through genetic evolution. Genetic mutations that are beneficial in a particular environment can increase in frequency in a population over time, leading to evolutionary changes in the species. For example, the evolution of the peppered moth is a classic example of genetic adaptation. Prior to the Industrial Revolution, the light-colored form of the moth was more common because it blended in with the lichen-covered bark of trees. However, as pollution darkened the bark, the dark-colored form became more common because it was better camouflaged. This shift in the frequency of different color morphs was driven by natural selection.

Sure, here is more body content for the research paper on "How do plants and animals adapt to their environments, and what role does evolution play?"

One major way that plants and animals adapt to their environments is through natural selection, which is a key mechanism of evolution. Natural selection is the process by which certain traits become more or less common in a population over time, depending on how those traits affect the individual's ability to survive and reproduce in their environment. This can lead to the evolution of new species or subspecies over time, as populations diverge in response to different environmental pressures.

For example, one well-known example of plant adaptation is the evolution of drought-resistant succulents in arid regions. These plants have adapted to survive in dry environments by storing water in their leaves and stems, and by reducing the size of their leaves to minimize water loss through transpiration. In contrast, plants in wetter environments may have larger leaves to capture more sunlight for photosynthesis, and may not need to store as much water.

Animals also show a wide range of adaptations to their environments. For example, some animals have developed camouflage to blend in with their surroundings and avoid predation, while others have developed warning colors to signal to predators that they are toxic or dangerous. Other animals may have adapted to specific diets or habitats, such as herbivores that have specialized teeth and digestive systems for breaking down tough plant material.

Adaptation is not always a smooth process, and it involves both advantages and disadvantages. For example, certain physical adaptations can restrict an animal's movement or make it more visible to predators, while certain behavioral adaptations can take a significant amount of energy to perform. However, organisms that do not adapt to their environment eventually face extinction.

The process of evolution plays a significant role in how plants and animals adapt to their environments. Evolution is the change in the genetic composition of a population over time, resulting in a change in the characteristics of a species. The process of evolution is driven by natural selection, which is the process by which organisms with advantageous traits are more likely to survive and reproduce. Over time, these advantageous traits become more prevalent in the population, while the traits that are not as advantageous become less common.

One example of adaptation and evolution is the camouflage of animals in their environment. For example, chameleons have the ability to change their color to blend in with their surroundings, which helps them to avoid predators. In addition, many species of birds have developed coloration and patterns that help them to blend in with their environment, which makes it difficult for predators to spot them. Similarly, many plants have developed adaptations to survive in specific environments. For example, desert plants have developed the ability to store water, while aquatic plants have developed adaptations to absorb nutrients from the water.

One of the most fascinating aspects of adaptation and evolution is the role of genetics. Adaptation to new environments can involve changes in the genetic makeup of a population, and over time, these genetic changes can lead to the emergence of new species. The process of evolution is driven by natural selection, where individuals with beneficial traits are more likely to survive and reproduce, passing those traits onto their offspring.

Genetic variation is the key to adaptation and evolution. It is the raw material upon which natural selection acts. Without genetic variation, there can be no adaptation, as there is nothing to select. Genetic variation can arise in a number of ways, including mutation, recombination, and gene flow. Mutation is the ultimate source of genetic variation, as it creates new alleles (versions of genes) that were not present in the population before. Recombination and gene flow can also introduce new combinations of alleles into a population, allowing for new traits to emerge.

Adaptation is not always a simple process, as it can involve trade-offs between different traits. For example, a bird with a longer beak may be better at obtaining food from deep flowers, but may also be more vulnerable to predators. Natural selection must strike a balance between these different pressures, resulting in organisms that are adapted to their specific environments.

The study of adaptation and evolution has important practical applications, such as in conservation biology and agriculture. Understanding how populations adapt to changing environments can help us predict how they will respond to climate change, habitat destruction, and other environmental challenges. In agriculture, knowledge of adaptation and evolution can be used to develop crop varieties that are better suited to local conditions, leading to higher yields and more sustainable farming practices.

There are various mechanisms by which plants and animals adapt to their environments. For instance, animals may evolve to better camouflage themselves against predators or develop enhanced sensory abilities to detect prey. Similarly, plants can evolve adaptations to their environment, such as drought tolerance or nutrient uptake efficiency. These adaptations are largely the result of natural selection and genetic variations within a population.

In the case of animals, evolution plays a crucial role in driving adaptation. Genetic variations can arise through mutation, recombination, and gene flow, among other processes. Some of these variations may be beneficial, allowing certain individuals to better survive and reproduce in a given environment. Over time, these beneficial traits become more prevalent in the population, as individuals with these traits are more likely to pass them on to their offspring. Over many generations, these changes in the gene pool can lead to the emergence of new species or subspecies that are better adapted to their environments.

Plants also undergo evolution and adaptation through genetic variation and natural selection. For example, plants living in areas with low nutrient levels may evolve adaptations to better absorb nutrients from the soil, such as longer root systems or symbiotic relationships with fungi. Similarly, plants living in areas with low water availability may evolve drought tolerance mechanisms, such as the ability to store water or close stomata to prevent water loss.

In both cases, the adaptive traits are the result of complex interactions between genetic and environmental factors. However, the pace and extent of adaptation can vary depending on the severity and rate of environmental change. Rapid changes, such as those caused by climate change or habitat destruction, may limit the ability of organisms to adapt quickly enough, potentially leading to extinction. Understanding the mechanisms of adaptation and evolution can help inform conservation efforts and management strategies to protect and preserve biodiversity.

One interesting adaptation in plants is the evolution of carnivorous plants. These plants have adapted to low-nutrient environments by developing the ability to capture and digest small animals, such as insects. For example, the Venus flytrap (Dionaea muscipula) has modified leaves that form a trap when triggered by a prey item. Once the prey is captured, the plant secretes digestive enzymes to break down the animal and extract nutrients.

In addition to physical adaptations, animals have also evolved a variety of behavioral adaptations to survive in their environments. For example, many animals migrate to more hospitable environments to escape harsh weather conditions. Some species of birds, such as the Arctic tern, undertake some of the longest migrations of any animal, traveling up to 70,000 km in a year.

Another notable example of animal adaptation is the ability of some species to camouflage themselves. Camouflage allows animals to blend in with their surroundings, making it harder for predators to spot them. The chameleon is a classic example of an animal that has evolved this adaptation. Their skin changes color to match their environment, allowing them to blend in with their surroundings and avoid detection.

These adaptations are all the result of the process of evolution. Over time, genetic mutations occur in populations of organisms, leading to variations in physical and behavioral traits. When these traits confer a survival advantage, they are more likely to be passed on to the next generation. Through this process of natural selection, populations of plants and animals are able to adapt to their changing environments.

One example of animal adaptation is the development of wings in birds. The ancestors of modern birds were likely small, ground-dwelling dinosaurs that did not have wings. Over time, some of these dinosaurs evolved longer arms with feathers that may have helped them glide from trees or other high points. Eventually, wings evolved and allowed for powered flight, which was a major innovation that enabled birds to become one of the most diverse and widespread groups of animals on Earth.

Plants also have numerous adaptations that help them survive in different environments. For example, cacti have adapted to life in arid environments by developing thick, fleshy stems that can store water, and by reducing the size and number of leaves to minimize water loss through transpiration. Other plants have evolved mechanisms for coping with poor soil conditions, such as developing deep root systems to access water and nutrients, or by forming symbiotic relationships with soil bacteria or fungi that can help them absorb essential nutrients.

Evolution is the process by which populations of organisms change over time in response to changes in their environment. These changes can result in new adaptations and traits that help organisms survive and reproduce more successfully. The driving force behind evolution is natural selection, which is the process by which certain traits become more or less common in a population based on how well they help organisms survive and reproduce.

In conclusion, the ability of plants and animals to adapt to their environments is crucial for their survival and the maintenance of biodiversity. Evolutionary processes, such as natural selection, genetic drift, and gene flow, play a key role in driving these adaptations. By allowing organisms to adapt to changes in their environment over time, evolution has led to the incredible diversity of life on Earth today. However, human activities, such as habitat destruction and climate change, are putting immense pressure on many species and their ability to adapt. Therefore, understanding the mechanisms of adaptation and the role of evolution is essential for conservation efforts and the preservation of biodiversity

What is the origin and fate of the universe, and how does it relate to the concept of time?

Introduction:

The universe has been the subject of human curiosity for centuries, with many cultures and civilizations attempting to understand its origin, composition, and ultimate fate. This exploration has taken many forms, from philosophical speculation to empirical observation and scientific investigation. At the center of this inquiry lies the concept of time, a phenomenon that is intimately connected with the universe and its evolution. In this research paper, we will examine the current scientific understanding of the origin and fate of the universe and the relationship between these concepts and the concept of time.

The Big Bang Theory:
The most widely accepted scientific theory of the origin of the universe is the Big Bang Theory. According to this theory, the universe began as a singularity, an infinitely small and dense point in space-time. Approximately 13.8 billion years ago, this singularity expanded and rapidly cooled, leading to the formation of matter and energy and the eventual birth of the universe. This initial expansion was followed by billions of years of cooling and the formation of galaxies, stars, and eventually planets and life.

The Fate of the Universe:
The fate of the universe is a topic of much speculation and debate among scientists. One popular theory is that the universe will eventually stop expanding and start contracting, leading to a "Big Crunch." In this scenario, all matter and energy in the universe would eventually be re-compressed into a singularity, much like the one from which the universe is thought to have originated. Another theory is that the universe will continue to expand indefinitely, eventually becoming too diffuse and spread out to sustain life or support any meaningful physical interactions.

The Concept of Time:
Time is a central concept in our understanding of the universe and its evolution. The concept of time has been described in many ways, including as a dimension in space-time, as a progression of events, and as a subjective experience. In the context of the universe, time is closely linked to the concept of entropy or the measure of the disorder and randomness of a system. As the universe expands and evolves, it is thought to become increasingly disordered and random, moving from a more structured and ordered state in the past to a more chaotic and

disordered state in the future.

The study of the origin and fate of the universe has been a topic of great interest and fascination for centuries and has been the subject of much scientific and philosophical inquiry. One of the key questions in this area is how the universe began and what is its ultimate fate. The standard model of cosmology posits that the universe began as a singularity, a point of infinite density and temperature, approximately 13.8 billion years ago. From this singularity, the universe expanded and cooled rapidly, leading to the formation of matter and eventually the structure we see today.

One of the main challenges in understanding the universe is how to reconcile its apparent vastness with our limited understanding of physics. According to the theory of general relativity, the universe is expanding at an accelerating rate, and it is widely believed that it will eventually reach a state of maximum expansion before eventually collapsing in on itself. This concept is known as the "big rip." Another possibility is that the universe will continue to expand at a slower rate and eventually reach a state of "heat death," where all matter is evenly distributed and no further energy can be extracted.

The concept of time is closely tied to our understanding of the universe and its evolution. Time is a fundamental aspect of our experience, and is a crucial component of many physical laws. However, our understanding of time is limited, and there is an ongoing debate about its true nature. Some scientists believe that time is an emergent property of the universe, arising from the interactions of matter and energy. Others believe that time is a fundamental aspect of the universe, and that it exists independently of matter and energy.

One theory that seeks to explain the origin and fate of the universe is the Big Bang theory. According to this theory, the universe began as a singularity, a point of infinite density and temperature, approximately 13.8 billion years ago. From this singularity, the universe rapidly expanded and cooled, leading to the formation of matter and energy as we know it today.

However, despite the success of the Big Bang theory in explaining the origin of the universe, the fate of the universe is still a topic of ongoing debate and research. Some scientists believe that the universe will eventually stop expanding and collapse in on itself, leading to another singularity in a process known as the Big Crunch. Others believe that the expansion of the universe will continue indefinitely, leading to slow cooling and eventual heat death.

The relationship between the concept of time and the universe is a complex one, with scientists still seeking to understand how time fits into our understanding of the universe. Some physicists believe that time is a fundamental aspect of the universe, while others see it as a human construct used to understand the progression of events.

One of the major challenges in exploring the relationship between the universe and time is the fact that our understanding of the universe is limited by the speed of light. This means that we can only observe events that have taken place within a certain distance from us, and our understanding of the universe's history is limited to the brief moment in time that we have been able to observe.

Despite these challenges, the study of the universe and its relationship to time continues to be a source of fascination and intrigue for scientists and the general public alike. With advances in technology and a growing understanding of the fundamental laws of the universe, we can expect continued progress in our quest to understand the origin and fate of the universe and how it relates to the concept of time.

One of the key debates in cosmology today is whether the universe will continue to expand indefinitely or will eventually collapse in on itself. If the universe continues to expand, it will eventually become cold and dark, with all the stars and galaxies too far apart to interact with one another. This is known as the "heat death" of the universe. On the other hand, if the universe collapses, it will eventually reach a point of maximum density and temperature known as the "Big Crunch."

Despite our current understanding of the universe, there is still much we do not know about its origin and fate. The study of cosmology is still a relatively new field, and many unanswered questions require further investigation.

One such question is the nature of dark matter and dark energy, which make up a significant portion of the universe but have yet to be directly observed. Understanding the properties of these mysterious substances could help us better understand the dynamics of the universe and its ultimate fate.

Another area of ongoing research is the study of gravitational waves. The detection of these waves, which are ripples in the fabric of spacetime itself, has opened up a new window into the study of the universe. By observing the properties of these waves, scientists hope to gain new insights into the earliest moments of the universe and its ultimate fate.

The concept of time is also intricately connected to the origin and fate of the universe. According to the Big Bang theory, the universe began as a singularity, a point of infinite density and temperature, and has been expanding ever since. However, the universe's fate depends on the amount of matter it contains and the rate of expansion. If the universe contains enough matter, it will eventually stop expanding and start contracting, leading to a "Big Crunch," where everything will be compressed back into a singularity. On the other hand, if the universe does not contain enough matter, it will continue to expand indefinitely, eventually leading to a "Big Freeze" or "Heat Death," where everything will become cold and dark.

The concept of time also becomes complicated when considering the possibility of multiple universes or a multiverse. Some theories suggest that our universe is just one of many universes, each with different laws of physics and constants. This could mean that time behaves differently in other universes, or that there may be no "beginning" or "end" to the multiverse as a whole.

The observation of cosmic microwave background radiation has helped to corroborate the Big Bang theory, suggesting that the universe originated from a highly compressed point and has been expanding ever since. However, scientists still lack a complete understanding of the universe's origin and fate.

One of the main questions is whether the universe will continue to expand indefinitely or eventually contract into a "Big Crunch." The answer depends on the universe's density, with a critical density that would result in an expansion that slows down but never stops and a density greater than the critical density that would lead to a collapse. Recent observations have suggested that the universe's density is below the critical density, implying that the universe will continue to expand.

The fate of the universe is also related to the concept of time. The idea of the arrow of time, which refers to the one-way direction of time, is rooted in the second law of thermodynamics, which states that the total entropy of a closed system always increases over time. The entropy of the universe is believed to have been low at the time of the Big Bang and to have been increasing ever since. This suggests that time may only flow in one direction, from past to future.

According to current understanding, the expansion of the universe will continue to accelerate due to the presence of dark energy. This acceleration means that the universe will become increasingly diffuse and empty, with galaxies moving away from each other faster and faster. Eventually, the galaxies will move so far apart that they will no longer be visible from each other, and the night sky will be dark.

While the ultimate fate of the universe is still unknown, some theories suggest that the universe will continue to expand forever, while others predict a "Big Crunch" in which the universe will eventually collapse in on itself. In either case, the concept of time will be intimately tied to the fate of the universe.

If the universe continues to expand indefinitely, then time will continue to progress in the same way that it does now, with the flow of time being determined by the movement of matter and energy in the universe. However, if the universe collapses in on itself, then time as we know it will come to an end.

At the moment of the Big Crunch, the universe will become incredibly dense and hot, with all matter and energy compressed into a tiny point. At this point, the laws of physics as we know them will break down, and it will be impossible to predict what will happen next. Some theories suggest that the universe will "bounce back" and begin expanding again in a new Big Bang, while others suggest that the universe will be destroyed completely.

In either case, the fate of the universe is intimately tied to the concept of time, and our understanding of time is inextricably linked to our understanding of the universe. While many questions about the origin and fate of the universe remain unanswered, scientists continue to explore these fundamental questions to deepen our understanding of the world around us.

One of the most intriguing concepts in cosmology is the multiverse theory. According to this theory, the universe is not unique and there are other universes besides our own. These universes may have different physical constants, laws of physics, and dimensions. The multiverse theory has been proposed as a solution to the question of why our universe appears to be so finely tuned for life. If there are an infinite number of universes, then it is not surprising that at least one universe would be hospitable to life.

However, the multiverse theory is highly speculative and there is currently no direct evidence to support it. It is difficult to test because, by definition, we can only observe our universe. Nevertheless, it is a topic of much research and debate in the field of cosmology.

Another fascinating aspect of the origin and fate of the universe is the concept of time. Time is a fundamental aspect of our experience of the world, but the nature of time is still not well understood. One of the most important questions is whether the time is absolute or relative. In the theory of relativity, time is relative to the observer's frame of reference. This means that time can appear to move slower or faster depending on the observer's velocity and proximity to massive objects.

There is also the question of whether the time is continuous or discrete. In classical physics, time is assumed to be continuous and infinitely divisible. However, in quantum mechanics, time is treated as a discrete variable that is divided into tiny units. The nature of time is closely related to the concept of causality and the arrow of time. The arrow of time refers to the fact that time only moves in one direction, from the past to the future. This is related to the second law of thermodynamics, which states that the entropy (disorder) of a closed system always increases over time.

Understanding the origin and fate of the universe and the nature of time is one of the greatest challenges of modern science. It requires a deep understanding of physics, mathematics, and philosophy. While we have made remarkable progress in our understanding of the universe, there is still much to learn and discover. The quest to understand the universe and our place in it is one of the most fundamental and awe-inspiring endeavors of human knowledge.

Current theories of the origin and fate of the universe are based on our current understanding of physics and cosmology. Despite the remarkable progress that has been made in these fields, many questions remain unanswered, and discoveries continue to challenge our current understanding.

One of the most significant challenges in understanding the origin of the universe is the problem of cosmic inflation. According to the standard model of cosmology, the universe underwent a period of rapid expansion immediately after the Big Bang, during which it expanded by a factor of at least 10^{78} in less than a second. This inflationary period is believed to be responsible for the uniformity and isotropy of the universe, but its underlying cause remains a mystery.

Another area of active research is the study of dark matter and dark energy. Dark matter is a form of matter that does not interact with light and has not been directly observed, but its presence is inferred from its gravitational effects on visible matter. Dark energy is even more mysterious and is believed to be responsible for the observed accelerated expansion of the universe.

The concept of time also plays a crucial role in our understanding of the universe's origin and fate. The Big Bang theory suggests that the universe began as a singularity, a point of infinite density and temperature, around 13.8 billion years ago. However, the singularity concept raises the question of what came before the Big Bang and what conditions were present at that time.

Moreover, the concept of time itself is not well understood in the context of the universe's early moments. Our current understanding of time is based on the concept of entropy, which describes the gradual decay of systems toward a state of maximum disorder. However, during the early moments of the universe's existence, the laws of physics were very different, and our understanding of time may not be applicable.

In terms of the fate of the universe, there are several possibilities. One scenario is that the universe will continue to expand indefinitely, eventually cooling to the point where all matter is dispersed and the universe becomes cold and dark. Another possibility is the Big Crunch, in which the universe eventually stops expanding and begins to contract until it collapses back into a singularity. Some theories suggest that the universe may undergo a cyclical process of expansion and contraction, in which each cycle begins with a new Big Bang.

One of the most intriguing and puzzling concepts related to the origin and fate of the universe is the possibility of a multiverse. The idea of a multiverse suggests that there could be an infinite number of universes, each with its unique physical laws and properties. This concept arises from the idea that our universe may be just one among many possible universes, and that each of these universes could have formed from different initial conditions and evolved differently over time.

The concept of a multiverse has been proposed as a way to explain some of the peculiarities of our universe, such as the fine-tuning of physical constants and the apparent existence of dark matter and energy. However, the idea of a multiverse is still a matter of debate and speculation, and there is currently no direct empirical evidence to support it.

Another concept that relates to the origin and fate of the universe is the concept of time. Time is a fundamental aspect of our experience of the world, but the nature of time is still a matter of philosophical and scientific debate. Some theories of physics suggest that time may be an emergent property of the universe, arising from the interactions between particles and fields. Other theories suggest that time may be an illusion and that the universe exists in a timeless, static state.

The relationship between the origin and fate of the universe and the concept of time is also related to the question of whether the universe is deterministic or probabilistic. If the universe is deterministic, then the future is determined by the present and the past, and the concept of free will may be illusory. If the universe is probabilistic, then the future is uncertain and open, and free will may be a real aspect of human experience.

These questions about the origin and fate of the universe, and the nature of time, are some of the deepest and most fascinating questions that humans have ever asked. Although we may never have complete answers to these questions, the search for knowledge and understanding is an important part of what makes us human.

CHAPTER SEVEN

How do different forms of energy, such as light and heat, interact with each other?

Energy is the capacity to do work, and there are various forms of energy, such as light, heat, sound, kinetic, and potential energy. Light and heat are two forms of energy that are closely related and have various applications in our daily lives. The interaction between these two forms of energy is a crucial topic of study that can provide a better understanding of the physical and chemical processes that govern our world. This research paper will explore the interaction between light and heat, including the physics and chemistry behind their interaction, their applications in various fields, and the future possibilities of this research.

Physics of Light and Heat Interaction:

Light and heat are both forms of energy that are propagated through waves. Light waves have a higher frequency and shorter wavelength, whereas heat waves have a lower frequency and longer wavelength. When light interacts with matter, it can be absorbed, transmitted, or reflected. The amount of light absorbed or reflected by an object depends on its color, texture, and the angle of incidence. When light is absorbed by an object, it is converted into heat energy. The heat energy generated by the absorption of light is proportional to the intensity of the light, the surface area of the object, and the time it is exposed to the light.

The absorption of light by matter is governed by the laws of quantum mechanics. At the atomic level, electrons absorb light energy, which causes them to jump to a higher energy level. The absorbed energy is then released as heat when the electrons return to their original energy level. The energy released as heat is directly proportional to the amount of light absorbed by the electrons. The interaction between light and matter is essential in various fields, including optics, photovoltaics, and photochemistry.

Chemistry of Light and Heat Interaction:

The interaction between light and heat is not limited to the physical domain. Light energy can also be used to trigger chemical reactions. This process is known as photochemistry. Photochemical reactions occur when light energy is absorbed by a molecule, which causes it to undergo a chemical transformation. The energy required to initiate the reaction is supplied by the absorbed light energy.

The absorption of light by molecules is governed by their electronic structure. Molecules with unsaturated bonds, such as double and triple bonds, absorb light energy in the ultraviolet region of the spectrum. The energy absorbed by these molecules can be used to break the unsaturated bonds and initiate a chemical reaction. The products of photochemical reactions can have various applications, including the synthesis of drugs, materials, and fuels.

Applications of Light and Heat Interaction:

The interaction between light and heat has various applications in our daily lives. In the field of optics, the reflection and refraction of light are used to create lenses, mirrors, and prisms. These devices are used in various optical instruments, including telescopes, cameras, and microscopes. The absorption of light energy by matter is the principle behind photovoltaic cells, which are used to convert sunlight into electricity. The energy released as heat by the absorption of light is also used in various applications, including cooking, heating, and drying.

The interaction between light and matter is also essential in the field of photochemistry. Photochemical reactions have applications in the synthesis of drugs, materials, and fuels. For example, the synthesis of vitamin D, an essential nutrient for humans, is initiated by a photochemical reaction in the skin when it is exposed to sunlight. The use of light energy to trigger chemical reactions has the potential to revolutionize the way we synthesize chemicals and materials.

Future Possibilities:

The interaction between light and heat is a rapidly evolving field of research that has the potential to provide solutions to various global challenges, including climate change, energy production, and healthcare. The development of new materials that can efficiently absorb and convert sunlight into electricity is a critical area of research

One of the most significant interactions between light and heat is the phenomenon of absorption. When light energy is absorbed by an object, it is converted into heat energy. The absorbed light energy excites the atoms and molecules of the object, causing them to vibrate and generate heat. This is the principle behind the functioning of solar panels, which absorb light energy and convert it into electrical energy.

Another important interaction between light and heat is reflection. When light hits an object, it can either be absorbed, transmitted, or reflected. The amount of light reflected by an object depends on its surface properties, such as its texture and color. Dark-colored and rough surfaces tend to absorb more light and heat, while light-colored and smooth surfaces tend to reflect more light and heat.

Conversely, the process of radiation involves the emission of energy in the form of heat and light. All objects emit radiation, which is a result of the thermal energy of their molecules. The amount of radiation emitted depends on the temperature of the object, with hotter objects emitting more radiation. This principle is used in infrared cameras, which detect the radiation emitted by objects to produce images based on the temperature variations.

In addition to absorption, reflection, and radiation, light and heat can also interact through the process of convection. Convection is the transfer of heat through the movement of fluids, such as air or water. When a fluid is heated, it expands and becomes less dense, causing it to rise. As it rises, it carries heat energy with it, which can be transferred to other objects or areas.

The interaction of light and heat energy has significant implications in many areas, including materials science, optics, and energy production. The behavior of light and heat in these fields can be complex, and understanding their interaction is important for developing new materials and technologies that can better utilize energy.

In materials science, light and heat can cause changes in the properties of materials. For example, when light is absorbed by a material, it can cause the electrons in the material to become excited and move to a higher energy state. This can lead to changes in the electrical, magnetic, and optical properties of the material. Similarly, heat can cause changes in the structure of materials by breaking or forming bonds between atoms.

In optics, the interaction of light and heat is crucial for designing devices such as lasers and fiber-optic cables. In a laser, a medium is stimulated with light, which causes it to emit a coherent beam of light. The intensity and wavelength of the emitted light are determined by the properties of the medium, and how it interacts with the incoming light. In fiber-optic cables, light is transmitted through a long, thin strand of glass or plastic. The amount of light that is lost as it travels through the cable depends on the material properties and the temperature of the cable.

Finally, the interaction of light and heat has important implications in energy production. For example, solar cells convert light into electrical energy, and the efficiency of this conversion depends on how the cells interact with light. Similarly, in power plants, heat is used to generate steam, which drives a turbine to produce electricity. The efficiency of this process depends on how well the heat is transferred to the water, and how much of the heat is lost as it moves through the system.

Light and heat are two forms of energy that are closely related and can interact with each other in various ways. One of the primary ways that light and heat interact is through the process of absorption. When an object absorbs light energy, it can convert that energy into heat energy. For example, when sunlight hits a dark surface, the surface absorbs the light, which then raises the temperature of the surface and causes it to emit heat.

Another way that light and heat can interact is through reflection. When light strikes a reflective surface, it can be reflected back, which can cause the surface to heat up. For example, when sunlight reflects off a mirror and onto a surface, the surface can absorb some of the reflected light and convert it into heat energy.

Conversely, when heat is applied to a material, it can cause the material to emit light energy. This is known as incandescence and is commonly seen in light bulbs. When an electric current is passed through a filament in a light bulb, the filament heats up and emits light energy as a result.

In addition to absorption, reflection, and incandescence, light and heat can also interact through other physical and chemical processes. For example, certain chemical reactions can produce light and heat energy as byproducts, such as the combustion of fossil fuels.

Understanding the interactions between different forms of energy is essential for a variety of scientific and technological applications, from developing more efficient energy systems to designing advanced materials with specific optical and thermal properties. Further research in this area is necessary to fully understand the complex interactions between light and heat and to develop new technologies and materials that can take advantage of these interactions in innovative ways.

Light and heat are two distinct forms of energy that have different properties, yet they interact in various ways. One of the most common ways that they interact is through radiation, which refers to the emission and absorption of energy in the form of electromagnetic waves.

Radiation is the process by which energy is transmitted through space and materials. Light, which is a form of electromagnetic radiation, is emitted by sources such as the sun and light bulbs, and can be absorbed, transmitted, or reflected by different materials. Heat, on the other hand, is the energy associated with the movement of molecules in a substance, and can be transferred from one substance to another through conduction, convection, or radiation.

One way in which light and heat interact is through the absorption of light by materials, which can result in the conversion of light energy into heat energy. This is the principle behind the greenhouse effect, in which the Earth's atmosphere traps some of the heat from the sun, keeping the planet warm enough to support life. Similarly, solar panels work by absorbing light energy and converting it into electrical energy.

Another way in which light and heat interact is through reflection. When light strikes a surface, it can be reflected back or absorbed, depending on the properties of the surface. Some materials, such as mirrors, are highly reflective and can reflect nearly all of the light that strikes them. Other materials, such as black asphalt, are highly absorbent and can convert most of the light energy into heat.

In addition to radiation, light and heat can also interact through the process of convection, which is the transfer of heat by the movement of fluids. For example, the heat from the sun causes the air near the Earth's surface to warm up, which causes it to rise and create convection currents. These currents can have a significant impact on weather patterns and can even cause natural disasters such as hurricanes and tornadoes.

Energy comes in many different forms and can interact with each other in various ways. One of the most common interactions is between light and heat energy. Light energy can be converted into heat energy when it is absorbed by a material. This is why dark-colored objects tend to get hotter in the sun than light-colored objects, as they absorb more light energy.

Another way that different forms of energy can interact is through the conversion of one form of energy into another. For example, solar panels convert light energy from the sun into electrical energy that can be used to power homes and businesses. Similarly, wind turbines convert kinetic energy from the wind into electrical energy.

Energy can also be transferred from one object to another through a process called conduction. In this process, heat energy is transferred from a hotter object to a cooler object when the two objects are in contact with each other. This is why a metal spoon left in a hot cup of tea will eventually become hot as well.

In addition, energy can be transferred through convection, which occurs when heat energy is transferred by the movement of a fluid or gas. This is why warm air rises and cool air sinks, and why ocean currents are created.

In addition to the interaction between light and heat, other forms of energy can also interact with each other. For example, electrical energy and magnetic energy can interact to produce electromagnetic waves, which include visible light, radio waves, and X-rays. These waves can be described as both waves of electric and magnetic energy oscillating at right angles to each other.

Another example is the interaction between kinetic energy and potential energy. Kinetic energy is the energy of motion, while potential energy is the energy of position or state. When an object is lifted to a certain height, it gains potential energy, which can be converted to kinetic energy when it is released and falls back down.

The interaction between different forms of energy is also important in many natural phenomena, such as weather patterns and geological processes. For example, the interaction between heat energy, water vapor, and air pressure can lead to the formation of thunderstorms and hurricanes. In the Earth's crust, the interaction between thermal energy and pressure can cause rocks to deform and create geological features such as mountains and faults.

Understanding the interactions between different forms of energy is essential for many areas of science and technology, from developing renewable energy sources to designing more efficient engines and power systems. It also has important implications for environmental and climate science, as the interplay between different forms of energy is a major driver of weather patterns and global climate change.

As our understanding of the interactions between different forms of energy continues to evolve, we can expect to see many new technological innovations and scientific breakthroughs that will transform the way we harness and utilize energy. These innovations will not only improve our quality of life but also help to address many of the pressing challenges facing our planet today, from climate change to resource depletion and environmental degradation.

The way different forms of energy interact with each other can have profound effects on the natural world. For example, the absorption of light energy by plants is a critical process that allows them to photosynthesize and produce the energy they need to survive. However, if too much light energy is absorbed, it can lead to photooxidative damage and ultimately death. This is why plants have evolved various protective mechanisms to dissipate excess energy and prevent damage, such as non-photochemical quenching.

In addition to light, heat is another important form of energy that interacts with the natural world. Heat energy is responsible for driving many physical and chemical processes, such as the movement of fluids and the breakdown of complex molecules. Heat energy can also be exchanged between different systems, such as between the atmosphere and the oceans, which can have significant effects on climate and weather patterns.

One important aspect of how different forms of energy interact with each other is the concept of energy conversion. This refers to the process of transforming one form of energy into another. For example, photosynthesis converts light energy into chemical energy, while the burning of fossil fuels converts chemical energy into heat energy. Understanding these energy conversion processes is critical for developing sustainable energy technologies that minimize environmental impact.

When light is absorbed, it is converted into heat energy, and when heat is generated, it often results in the emission of light energy. This is the concept of thermoluminescence, where heat energy is absorbed by a material, and this energy excites the electrons to emit light energy. Another form of energy that interacts with light and heat is sound energy, which can be produced through the vibration of particles. When sound waves travel through a medium, they create pressure waves that can cause particles to move back and forth, producing heat and light energy.

The interaction between different forms of energy, such as light and heat, is an important aspect of energy transfer in various physical, chemical, and biological processes. For example, photosynthesis is a process where light energy is converted into chemical energy, while heat energy is used to break chemical bonds and create new ones. The conversion of light energy into heat energy can be seen in the process of solar radiation, where the sun's light energy is absorbed by the Earth's atmosphere, causing the air to heat up and produce heat energy.

There are many different types of energy, including light, heat, chemical, mechanical, and electrical energy. These forms of energy can interact with each other in various ways, depending on the situation.

One common way that energy interacts is through the process of conversion. For example, when light hits a solar panel, it is converted into electrical energy that can be used to power a device. Similarly, when a fuel is burned, the chemical energy in the fuel is converted into heat energy, which can then be used to generate electricity or provide heat for a building.

Another way that energy interacts is through the process of transfer. Heat is a common form of energy that is often transferred between objects or substances. For example, when a hot cup of coffee is placed on a table, the heat from the coffee is transferred to the table, warming it up. Heat can also be transferred through radiation, such as when the sun warms the Earth's surface.

In some cases, energy can also be stored and released over time. For example, a battery stores chemical energy that can be released as electrical energy when it is connected to a device. Similarly, a hot rock can store thermal energy that can be released slowly over time as it cools down.

Understanding how different forms of energy interact is important for many areas of science and technology. By studying these interactions, scientists can develop more efficient energy conversion and storage technologies, as well as better ways to harness and use energy from renewable sources like solar and wind power.

Light and heat are two of the most common forms of energy, and their interactions are crucial to many natural and technological processes. For example, the conversion of light energy into heat is the basis of solar heating and photothermal processes, while the conversion of heat energy into light is the basis of incandescent lighting. In addition, the interaction between light and heat plays an important role in atmospheric and climate processes, including the absorption and emission of radiation by greenhouse gases and the formation of clouds.

The interaction between light and heat can also lead to interesting and useful phenomena in materials science. For example, the photo-thermal effect, which is the absorption of light by a material that then produces heat, can be used for a range of applications, including photothermal therapy for cancer treatment and the production of photovoltaic cells for solar energy conversion. Another example is the thermophotovoltaic effect, where the conversion of heat into light is used to produce electricity.

Understanding the interactions between different forms of energy is essential for the development of new technologies and for understanding natural phenomena. Advances in our understanding of these interactions have already led to many important applications, and will likely continue to do so in the future. Ongoing research is exploring new ways to harness and control the interactions between light and heat, such as in the development of nanoscale photonic and thermal devices, and in the development of new materials for energy conversion and storage.

In addition, the interaction between light and heat is a crucial aspect in various industrial processes. For example, in the field of materials science, the interaction between light and heat can be utilized to synthesize new materials with unique properties. The use of light and heat can lead to the development of new applications, such as the creation of energy-efficient materials for buildings, advanced sensors, and high-performance electronic devices.

When considering the interactions between light and heat energy, it is important to understand how they are related. Heat is a form of energy that is transferred from one object to another due to a temperature difference, while light is a form of energy that travels in waves and can be absorbed, reflected, or transmitted by matter.

One of the ways that light and heat energy interact is through the absorption of light by matter. When light energy is absorbed, it can increase the temperature of the absorbing object, which is why dark-colored objects tend to absorb more heat than light-colored objects. This process is the basis for solar heating, where solar radiation is absorbed by a material and converted into heat energy.

Another way that light and heat energy interact is through the emission of light by heated objects. When an object is heated, it emits light in the form of electromagnetic radiation. The amount and wavelength of the emitted light depends on the temperature of the object. This is the basis for incandescent light bulbs, where a wire filament is heated until it emits visible light.

In addition to absorption and emission, light and heat energy can also be converted from one form to another. For example, a light bulb converts electrical energy into light and heat energy. Similarly, a solar panel converts solar energy into electrical energy.

The interactions between light and heat energy are important to a variety of fields, including materials science, engineering, and environmental science. Understanding how these forms of energy interact can help in the design of more efficient heating and cooling systems, as well as more effective solar panels and lighting technologies.